cooking with

GREEK YOGURT

cooking with

GREEK YOGURT

Healthy Recipes for Buffalo Blue Cheese Chicken, Greek Yogurt Pancakes, Mint Julep Frozen Yogurt, and More!

cassie johnston

THE COUNTRYMAN PRESS · WOODSTOCK, VT.

Published by The Countryman Press, P.O. Box 748,
Woodstock, VT 05091

Distributed by W. W. Norton & Company, Inc.,
500 Fifth Avenue, New York, NY 10110
Printed in the United States of America

Cooking with Greek Yogurt
ISBN 978-1-58157-239-1

10 9 8 7 6 5 4 3 2 1

to my readers + blends

THANK YOU FOR TEACHING ME SO MUCH

contents

54 soups

82 mains

112 sides + snacks

136 desserts

preface

Seven years ago, I had a health wake-up call. I sat on the crinkly paper of a sterile examination room, tears welling up in my eyes, as my family doctor told me I was on the fast track to die young. I was twenty-three years old and had blood pressure and cholesterol levels normally only seen in a middle-aged man. I was eighty pounds overweight and had never met a fast-food joint I didn't like.

I'd seen doctors before who'd explained the risks of my fast food–loving, exercise-hating lifestyle before, but this doctor got through. This doctor told me I was going to die before I turned thirty if I didn't change my lifestyle. Theatrical? Yes, maybe. But it worked. And I'm thankful every day that my doctor had a flair for the dramatic.

I was recently married, and the thought of dying young and leaving my husband behind was more than just a remote possibility that lived in the depths of my deepest, darkest nightmares. Instead, it was a legitimate forecast of the future. Something had to change.

Over the next few years, my husband and I slowly made the transition from the common American diet of fast, processed food to a diet made up almost entirely of whole, real, slow foods. It wasn't a quick transition, but with every box of cookies we tossed away and every new vegetable we tried, we became healthier and healthier.

Now, closing in on a decade removed from that doctor's visit, my cholesterol and blood pressure are both excellent, my weight is under control, and I'm passionate about sharing the joy of cooking with healthy, real, and nutrient-dense ingredients. My husband and I now run a small hobby farm and grow bushels and bushels of fresh fruits and vegetables to help fuel our healthy eating habit. Eating real food changed my life, and I'd love everyone to get a chance to feel as good as I do.

There are a lot of powerful, nutritious ingredients that are staples in my kitchen, but few are as prevalent in my cooking as Greek yogurt. This thick, creamy, tangy cousin to regular yogurt has skyrocketed in popularity over the past few years thanks to its incredible taste, texture, and nutritional benefits. I love eating Greek yogurt (also known as strained yogurt) straight up with fruits, nuts, or other toppings, but Greek yogurt really shines when it is used in cooking. Lightening up recipes is easy with Greek yogurt. It can be substituted for a whole bevy of typical heavy ingredients in cooking and baking (see Simple Substitutions, page 22), without much change to the flavor or texture of the final dish. Guests will never guess that Spicy Penne with Shrimp (page 106) is made thick and creamy with low-calorie, high-protein Greek yogurt instead of heavy cream, or that Lemon Poppy Seed Cupcakes (page 149) are a healthier option for the dessert table—I promise!

In these pages, you'll find dozens of recipes like these tested in my own kitchen that are flavorful, nutritious, and use Greek yogurt in creative ways that go beyond just a bowl and spoon. I hope you enjoy each and every one of them. Thank you for letting me into your kitchen!

the basics

With the added popularity of Greek yogurt over the past few years, there is a lot of info floating around about this dairy-case staple. Before we dig into cooking, let's go over some basic stats.

HOW IS IT MADE?

Traditionally, Greek yogurt is simply regular yogurt (milk fermented with bacteria) that has been strained through a fine sieve or cheesecloth to remove the majority of the whey. Many of the major brands selling traditional Greek yogurt still use this method to produce their yogurt (albeit with much larger, industrialized straining machines).

To keep up with the modern demand for Greek yogurt, some manufacturers have taken to creating their yogurt by using thickening agents (such as cornstarch or tapioca) instead of traditional straining. To know which is which, check the ingredients—traditionally made Greek yogurt will list only milk and live cultures, while yogurt made with thickeners will list them.

WHAT MAKES IT BETTER?

Many health-minded people prefer Greek yogurt to regular yogurt because, while it has a similar calorie and fat breakdown, Greek yogurt has nearly twice the amount of protein as regular yogurt.

Why is protein so great? Because getting enough protein is an important aspect of protecting our bodies from illness, making sure our muscles recover quickly from injury, and keeping all the reactions running smoothly in our tissues. Protein is good for the body! But what I love most about eating lots of protein is that it keeps me from feeling hungry. After a protein-less meal, I'm hungry sometimes as soon as an hour afterward. The more protein, the longer my belly stays full and happy. And that's good news for someone trying to stick to a healthy diet.

It is important to remember that using Greek yogurt doesn't give you the freedom to go crazy and shovel down an entire pan of mac and cheese. All the recipes in this book are full of healthy, whole foods, but keep in mind that one of the most important aspects of maintaining a healthy diet is exercising portion control.

Yogurt Compared *(approximately; check labels for variations by brand)*

	GREEK YOGURT	REGULAR YOGURT
Calories	173	133
Fat	4.7g	3.3g
Carbohydrates	9.3g	16g
Protein	22.7g	10.7g

Per 8 ounces of plain, low-fat

FLAVORED OR PLAIN?

While flavored Greek yogurt might be tasty, it also tends to hide an ugly truth—many flavored yogurts are packed with artificial colors, flavors, and up to five teaspoons of sugar per serving. The healthiest bet is to stick with plain Greek yogurt. And if you're missing the sweet, fruity taste of your favorite flavored yogurt, try adding in fruit, honey, or if you're having a particularly rough day, chocolate chips.

All the recipes in this book use plain Greek yogurt only. I like to keep a tub or two of plain on hand for cooking, eating, and substituting (see Simple Substitutions, page 22). By sticking with plain yogurt, you have control over the sugars, flavors, and additives. More control is always a good thing to have in the kitchen.

CAN I MAKE IT MYSELF?

You sure can! In fact, if you're on a budget (and who isn't?), I recommend making it at home. Sure, it's convenient to just swing by the store and pick up a tub, but at nearly double the cost of regular yogurt—triple if you want organic—it adds up quickly.

To make your own Greek yogurt, start by layering multiple layers of clean cheesecloth in a colander over a large bowl. Pour a tub of your favorite plain regular yogurt into the cheesecloth, stash it in the fridge, and let the yogurt drain until it reaches the desired consistency—I like to let it drain overnight. If cheesecloth is a little too messy for you, there are many tools out there on the market for straining yogurt.

For every cup of regular yogurt, expect to get about 2/3 cup Greek yogurt and 1/3 cup whey. Don't toss that whey! Whey has a ton of great kitchen uses. Sub it for buttermilk or other liquid when baking—it adds a nice sourdough taste. Add it to smoothies for a boost of protein and calcium. Use it instead of water to cook grains, rice, and pasta.

WHAT DO I NEED TO KNOW ABOUT COOKING WITH GREEK YOGURT?

In general, Greek yogurt is a pretty low-maintenance ingredient to cook with, but there are a few sticky situations to look out for:

High Temperatures: Greek yogurt tends to curdle when added to very high-temperature foods. The lower fat content in nonfat and low-fat versions is particularly problematic. Before adding Greek yogurt to a hot dish, test the temperature yourself. If it's too hot to eat, then it's too hot for Greek yogurt.

Vinegar-Based Dressings: Greek yogurt works as a great substitute for mayo or sour cream in a lot of vinegar-based dressings (such as what you'd use for slaw, potato salad, salad dressing, etc.) but it does tend to fall a little bit flat if you use 100 percent yogurt. I like to mix a small amount of the original ingredient with the Greek yogurt (see Simple Substitutions, page 22). A few tablespoons of mayo can go a long way to flavor dressings.

Freezing: Sometimes Greek yogurt tends to separate after freezing, but it's easily mixed back together by a vigorous stir or shake. I freeze soups with Greek yogurt in them all the time; often after they've defrosted, the soup looks curdled, but a quick stir and it's as good as new.

Find Your Favorite: If you don't plan on making your own Greek yogurt, make sure you do some shopping around to find your favorite brand. Each brand has their own method that produces pretty different flavors that will come through in many recipes. If you don't like a Greek yogurt brand on the spoon, you probably won't like it in a recipe either.

simple substitutions

If you're looking for a quick and easy way to lighten up one of your favorite recipes, Greek yogurt is the ingredient for you. Follow the formulas in the chart below to substitute Greek yogurt for some common ingredients.

	ORIGINAL	SUBSTITUTION
Sour Cream	1 cup	1 cup Greek yogurt
Oil (in baking)	1 cup	3/4 cup Greek yogurt
Butter	1 cup	1/2 cup (1 stick) butter + 1/4 cup Greek yogurt
Mayonnaise	1 cup	2 tablespoons mayo + 3/4 cup Greek yogurt
Cream Cheese	1 cup	1/4 cup cream cheese + 3/4 cup Greek yogurt

		ORIGINAL	SUBSTITUTION
	Buttermilk	1 cup	1/4 cup milk + 3/4 cup Greek yogurt
	Half-and-Half	1 cup	1/2 cup milk + 1/2 cup Greek yogurt
	Heavy Cream	1 cup	2/3 cup milk + 1/3 cup Greek yogurt
	Crème Fraîche	1 cup	1 cup Greek yogurt
	Regular Yogurt	1 cup	1/3 cup milk + 2/3 cup Greek yogurt
	Ricotta	1 cup	1/2 cup ricotta + 1/2 cup Greek yogurt

breakfasts

$\mathcal{O}$f all the meals in a day, the breakfast table is probably the most familiar with Greek yogurt. You'd be hard-pressed to find someone who hasn't grabbed a container of yogurt on the way out the door in the morning, but Greek yogurt's breakfast uses span way beyond the spoon.

When I first started eating healthier, one of my biggest struggles was getting in a nutritious breakfast every day. Sure, anyone can cook a healthy spread on a leisurely Sunday morning, but what about when the alarm didn't go off and you have five minutes to get out the door for work?

I've developed a portfolio of healthy breakfast recipes that are both tasty and speedy. You'll find quite a few of those in the next few pages, along with some of my slower Sunday morning favorites.

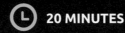 whole wheat greek yogurt
PANCAKES

This is the go-to pancake recipe in our house on Sunday mornings. These pancakes are packed with hearty whole grains, but stay light and fluffy thanks to the addition of Greek yogurt.

4 SERVINGS   **20 MINUTES**

INGREDIENTS

1 1/4 cups whole wheat flour

1 teaspoon baking powder

1/2 teaspoon ground cinnamon

1/4 teaspoon nutmeg

1/4 teaspoon salt

1 cup plain Greek yogurt

1/2 cup unsweetened applesauce

3 eggs

1/4 cup maple syrup

1/2 teaspoon vanilla extract

1/3 cup milk

DIRECTIONS

Preheat a griddle or large nonstick skillet over medium-high heat. In a large mixing bowl, mix together the flour, baking powder, cinnamon, nutmeg, and salt. In a small mixing bowl, whisk together the yogurt, applesauce, eggs, syrup, vanilla, and milk. Pour the liquid ingredients into the dry and mix until just combined. Let batter rest for 10 minutes.

Spoon 1/2 cup of the batter at a time onto the preheated griddle or skillet. Cook for 3 to 4 minutes, or until the edges of the pancake look solid, and bubbles begin to rise to the surface. Flip pancake and cook for 2 to 3 more minutes on the other side. Repeat with remaining batter.

Nutrition per 2 pancakes: 293 calories, 4g fat, 50g carbs, 13g protein

I love these pancakes topped with berries and maple syrup, but they're also great with melted peanut butter and a small smear of your favorite jam.

If peaches aren't in season in your area, this dish also works well with frozen peach slices. Just let them thaw on the counter or under warm water, and proceed just as you would with the fresh peaches.

peaches and cream STUFFED FRENCH TOAST

This luxe breakfast treat is perfect for houseguests and holiday breakfasts because it can be made ahead of time (in fact, it's better if you do!) and just popped into the oven that morning. Bring out the syrup and some plates, and breakfast is served.

 4 SERVINGS   **5 HOURS**

INGREDIENTS

8 slices thick-cut bread
4 ripe peaches, sliced thinly
1 1/2 cups plain Greek yogurt
3/4 cup milk
5 eggs

1/4 cup maple syrup
1 tablespoon vanilla extract
Pinch of salt
1 teaspoon ground cinnamon

DIRECTIONS

In a 9 x 13-inch pan, layer the bread and peach slices, then set aside. In a medium mixing bowl, whisk together the yogurt, milk, eggs, syrup, vanilla, salt, and cinnamon. Pour over the bread and peach slices, lifting the slices to help the mixture soak in. Wrap tightly with plastic wrap and let rest in the fridge for at least 4 hours, or overnight. In the morning, preheat oven to 350°. Remove plastic wrap and bake for 40 to 45 minutes, or until the top is golden brown and the custard is set.

Nutrition per 2 slices: 379 calories, 7g fat, 54g carbs, 20g protein

whole-grain blueberry
YOGURT MUFFINS

These lightly sweet whole-grain muffins are a great option for a grab-and-go breakfast. I like to make a big batch of these and keep them stashed in a zip-top bag in the freezer. After a few seconds in the microwave, they're just as good as eating them fresh out of the oven.

 16 MUFFINS   **35 MINUTES**

INGREDIENTS

2 cups whole wheat flour

1 cup all-purpose flour

1 tablespoon baking powder

1/2 teaspoon salt

1/2 cup (1 stick) butter, melted

2 large eggs

1 cup plain Greek yogurt

2/3 cup granulated sugar

1/2 cup low-fat milk

1 teaspoon vanilla extract

1 1/2 cups frozen blueberries

DIRECTIONS

Preheat oven to 375°. Line a muffin tin with paper muffin cups or spray with cooking spray, then set aside. In a large mixing bowl, whisk together the flours, baking powder, and salt, then set aside. In a medium mixing bowl, whisk together the melted butter, eggs, yogurt, sugar, milk, and vanilla extract. Pour the liquid ingredients into the flour mixture and stir until just barely combined—do not overmix. Carefully fold in the frozen blueberries until evenly distributed. Spoon batter into prepared muffin tin, filling the cups two-thirds full. Bake in preheated oven for 15 to 17 minutes, or until a toothpick inserted in the middle of the muffins comes out clean. Let cool for 5 minutes in muffin tin, then transfer to a cooling rack to cool completely.

Nutrition per muffin:
196 calories, 6.7g fat, 29.5g carbs, 4.8g protein

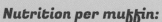

Leave out the blueberries,

and this muffin recipe makes a great base for all kinds of flavors. Some fun combos to try: dried cranberries and orange zest, chocolate chips and walnuts, coconut flakes and raspberries.

smoked salmon
EGGS BENEDICT

Thanks to an easy-to-make Greek yogurt hollandaise sauce, this eggs Benedict recipe is quick enough for even a busy weekday morning.

 4 SERVINGS   **20 MINUTES**

INGREDIENTS

2/3 cup plain Greek yogurt

1 teaspoon fresh lemon juice

2 egg yolks

1 teaspoon Dijon mustard

1/4 teaspoon granulated sugar

Pinch of salt

Pinch of black pepper

2 teaspoons minced fresh dill

8 ounces smoked salmon

4 English muffins, toasted

8 poached eggs

DIRECTIONS

In a heatproof bowl placed over a saucepan of simmering water, whisk together the yogurt, lemon juice, egg yolks, mustard, and sugar. Continue whisking for 10 minutes, or until the sauce has thickened and darkened. Remove from heat and whisk in the salt, pepper, and dill.

To assemble, layer 1 ounce of smoked salmon over each English muffin half, top with a poached egg, and drizzle with sauce.

Nutrition per serving: 383 calories, 16g fat, 27g carbs, 32g protein

Not into salmon?
For a vegetarian version, try swapping out the smoked salmon for sautéed spinach.

SMOKED SALMON
spread

This light spread is great as a dip or slathered on crackers, but it really shines atop a toasted bagel. Even folks who aren't big salmon fans enjoy this spread because it's so lightly flavored—no overwhelming fishiness here.

YOU'LL NEED

4 sprigs fresh dill

1/4 small onion

1 cup plain Greek yogurt

6 ounces cream cheese, softened

6 ounces smoked salmon

Pinch of salt and pepper

Nutrition per 2-tablespoon serving: 75 calories, 5g fat, 1g carbs, 5g protein

1 Finely mince the dill and onion.

2 Combine all ingredients in the basin of a food processor.

3 Pulse until spread is smooth.

4 Transfer spread to an airtight container and refrigerate for at least 2 hours to allow flavors to meld.

5 Serve on bagels or crackers.

I love this spread as a condiment on sandwiches (it's particularly good on a BLT).

tomato and herb
FRITTATA

A well-cooked frittata is nothing to be afraid of. It's easy, light, and incredibly tasty! Adding Greek yogurt to the mix keeps the eggs fluffy and tangy.

 **4 SERVINGS**    **30 MINUTES**

INGREDIENTS

1 tablespoon butter
1 cup cherry tomatoes, halved
6 eggs
1/3 cup plain Greek yogurt
Pinch of salt and pepper

2 tablespoons minced fresh parsley
2 tablespoons minced fresh oregano
2 tablespoons minced fresh basil
1/4 cup shredded Romano cheese

DIRECTIONS

Melt butter in a medium-sized ovenproof skillet over medium heat. Add in the tomatoes and cook until the tomatoes shrivel, about 5 minutes. Meanwhile, whisk together the eggs, yogurt, salt, and pepper. Once tomatoes have cooked, pour the egg mixture over them in the pan—do not stir. Reduce the heat to low and continue to cook over steady heat, using a plastic spatula to loosen the edge of the frittata occasionally.

Meanwhile, preheat the oven broiler. When the edges of the frittata are solid, but the middle is still slightly liquid, remove from heat, sprinkle with the herbs and cheese, and place under the broiler. Broil for 5 to 7 minutes, or until the frittata is set and the cheese is melted. Cut into 8 wedges for serving.

Nutrition per 2-wedge serving: 164 calories, 11g fat, 4g carbs, 12.3g protein

The star of this frittata is really the fragrant, fresh herbs. The combo here works great, but feel free to experiment and use whatever you have on hand.

overnight OATMEAL

B eing able to make food ahead of time is one of my favorite ways to make sure I stick to a healthy diet, and overnight oatmeal is one of my favorite make-ahead dishes. Overnight oatmeal is made without cooking and eaten cold, making it the perfect option for summer breakfast. The oats soak up liquid overnight in the fridge and leave you with a thick, creamy, delicious breakfast in the morning that requires no work other than pulling a spoon out of the utensil drawer. The possibilities for overnight oatmeal combinations are pretty much limitless, but these three are my absolute faves.

Chocolate-Raspberry Overnight Oatmeal

I think a great way to kick off a Monday morning is with a healthy breakfast that tastes almost like a dessert. It's impossible to have a bad day when you had chocolate for breakfast, I promise.

 1 SERVING **5 MINUTES (PLUS CHILLING TIME)**

INGREDIENTS

1/3 cup plain Greek yogurt

1/3 cup old-fashioned oats

1/2 teaspoon vanilla extract

Pinch of salt

2 tablespoons chocolate chips

1/3 cup fresh raspberries

1 tablespoon maple syrup

1/3 cup milk

DIRECTIONS

Combine all ingredients in a medium-sized mixing bowl—the mixture will be soupy. Transfer the oatmeal to an airtight container, and stash in the fridge for at least 4 hours or overnight. Eat cold.

Nutrition per serving: 366 calories, 10g fat, 55g carbs, 15g protein

Banana-Walnut Overnight Oatmeal

Banana bread and banana muffins are breakfast-time classics, but my favorite way to eat bananas in the a.m. is in overnight oatmeal. The banana adds sweetness and creaminess that is an awesome contrast to the tangy yogurt and crunchy, earthy walnuts.

 1 SERVING **5 MINUTES (PLUS CHILLING TIME)**

INGREDIENTS

1/3 cup plain Greek yogurt

1/3 cup old-fashioned oats

1/2 teaspoon vanilla extract

Pinch of salt

1 medium banana, sliced

2 tablespoons chopped walnuts

1 tablespoon maple syrup

1/3 cup milk

DIRECTIONS

Combine all ingredients in a medium-sized mixing bowl—the mixture will be soupy. Transfer the oatmeal to an airtight container, and stash in the fridge for at least 4 hours or overnight. Eat cold.

Nutrition per serving: 385 calories, 8.6g fat, 66g carbs, 15g protein

Carrot Cake Overnight Oatmeal

This oatmeal recipe not only tastes like a dessert but also helps you get your vegetables in! It's the best of both worlds.

 1 SERVING **5 MINUTES (PLUS CHILLING TIME)**

INGREDIENTS

1/3 cup plain Greek yogurt

1/3 cup old-fashioned oats

1/2 teaspoon vanilla extract

Pinch of salt

1 small carrot, peeled and shredded

Pinch of ground cinnamon

Pinch of ground cloves

2 tablespoons raisins

1 tablespoon maple syrup

1/3 cup milk

DIRECTIONS

Combine all ingredients in a medium-sized mixing bowl—the mixture will be soupy. Transfer the oatmeal to an airtight container, and stash in the fridge for at least 4 hours or overnight. Eat cold.

Nutrition per serving: 309 calories, 3.9g fat, 57g carbs, 13g protein

This recipe is a great crowd-pleaser and doubles or triples easily. You can even make it ahead of time, stash it in the fridge overnight and just bake in the morning. I like topping mine with a drizzle of warm maple syrup. Breakfast is served!

baked oatmeal with DATES AND PECANS

I love oatmeal in all forms, but there is something so perfectly warm and cozy about a pan of oatmeal that comes piping hot out of the oven on a weekend morning. I really like that the sweetness of this oatmeal comes from all-natural Medjool dates—not added sweeteners.

 4 SERVINGS   **40 MINUTES**

INGREDIENTS

8 Medjool dates, pitted and roughly chopped
1 cup old-fashioned oats
1/2 cup whole pecans
1/2 teaspoon baking powder
1 teaspoon ground cinnamon
Pinch of salt

1 cup milk
1/2 cup plain Greek yogurt
1 egg
2 tablespoons butter, melted
1 teaspoon vanilla extract

DIRECTIONS

Preheat oven to 375°. In a medium-sized mixing bowl, toss together the dates, oats, pecans, baking powder, cinnamon, and salt. Pour the oat mixture into an 8 x 8-inch baking dish, then set aside. In a small mixing bowl, whisk together the milk, yogurt, egg, butter, and vanilla until smooth. Pour the milk mixture over the oat mixture. Bake in preheated oven for 30 to 35 minutes, or until the mixture is browned and bubbly.

Nutrition per serving: 463 calories, 19g fat, 82g carbs, 11g protein

cranberry-oat
BREAKFAST BARS

These bars combine all the best of breakfast into a handheld meal. Whole grains, lean protein, and tasty dried cranberries come together to make a treat that tastes great on the go.

 24 BARS **45 MINUTES**

INGREDIENTS

1 1/2 cups old-fashioned oats

1 cup whole wheat flour

1/2 teaspoon baking soda

1/2 teaspoon salt

1/3 cup packed brown sugar

2 eggs

1/2 cup (1 stick) butter, melted

1/4 cup maple syrup

2 tablespoons milk

3/4 cup plain Greek yogurt

2 tablespoons all-purpose flour

1/2 cup granulated sugar

1 teaspoon vanilla extract

1 2/3 cups dried cranberries

DIRECTIONS

Preheat oven to 350°. Line a 9 x 13-inch pan with parchment paper and set aside.

To make the crust: In a medium mixing bowl, combine the oats, whole wheat flour, baking soda, salt, and brown sugar. In a separate small mixing bowl, combine one of the eggs, butter, maple syrup, and milk. Mix the wet ingredients with the dry. Reserve 1/2 cup of the crust mixture. Press the remaining crust mixture into the bottom of the prepared pan using damp, clean hands.

To prepare the topping: Whisk the remaining egg, yogurt, all-purpose flour, sugar, and vanilla together until smooth. Fold in the cranberries. Spread the topping over the crust. Sprinkle with reserved crust mixture. Bake in preheated oven for 20 to 25 minutes, or until the crust is golden brown. Let cool completely before slicing.

Nutrition per bar: 119 calories, 5g fat, 17g carbs, 2g protein

Quin-what?

Quinoa (pronounced keen-wah) is a whole grain that has gained a lot of popularity in recent years—for good reason. Quinoa is one of the few sources of complete vegetarian protein, meaning it includes all nine amino acids that your body needs to get from food sources. That makes quinoa one great grain to add to your breakfast! It's also quite tasty.

raspberry-coconut quinoa BREAKFAST PUDDING

Pudding for breakfast? Yup! This pudding tastes like a dessert but is packed with the nutritional value of a good, hearty breakfast. You can find coconut milk in the international foods aisle, but feel free to sub in soy, nut, or cow's milk if that's all you have on hand.

 4 SERVINGS   **20 MINUTES**

INGREDIENTS

1 cup quinoa

1 (14 ounce) can of light coconut milk

1/2 cup water

1/3 cup granulated sugar or honey

2 teaspoons vanilla extract

Pinch of salt

1/2 cup plain Greek yogurt

1 cup fresh raspberries

DIRECTIONS

In a medium saucepan over medium-high heat, combine the quinoa, coconut milk, water, and sugar or honey. Bring to a boil, reduce heat, and simmer for 12 to 15 minutes, or until all the liquid is absorbed. Remove from heat and let cool for 5 minutes, then stir in vanilla, salt, and yogurt. Divide into serving bowls and top with raspberries.

Nutrition per serving: *309 calories, 8g fat, 48g carbs, 8g protein*

super SMOOTHIES

Greek yogurt is a superstar addition to your favorite fruit smoothie. It's packed with belly-filling protein that'll help keep you satisfied long after your smoothie glass is empty. These three staple combinations are a great starting point, but feel free to get creative with your blender. Use a cup of Greek yogurt as your base and add in your favorite fruits to make your own personal super smoothie

Apple Pie Spinach Smoothie

This smoothie tastes just like the classic dessert but has a not-so-hidden secret—it's packed with spinach! The dark, leafy greens add a ton of nutrition, but their earthy flavor is masked with the incredible flavor of apples and cinnamon.

 1 SERVING **5 MINUTES**

INGREDIENTS

1/2 cup low-fat milk

1/2 cup apple juice

1/2 cup unsweetened applesauce

1 cup fresh spinach

1/2 cup plain Greek yogurt

1 banana

Pinch of ground cinnamon

A few ice cubes

DIRECTIONS

Combine all ingredients in the jar of a high-speed blender. Blend until very smooth.

Nutrition per serving: 325 calories, 2g fat, 66g carbs, 15g protein

Don't fear the green!

Some folks might be turned off by the green tint of this smoothie, but trust me, it doesn't taste spinachy. If it makes you feel better, you can just think of it as green apple–flavored.

Four-Berry Antioxidant Blast Smoothie

Dark-skinned berries are full of antioxidants that help protect your cells from the effects of free radicals—molecules produced in your body that are thought to play a role in increasing your risk of heart disease, cancer, and other diseases. Get your fill of antioxidants with this berry-packed smoothie.

1 SERVING   **5 MINUTES**

INGREDIENTS
1 cup plain Greek yogurt
1 banana
1/3 cup frozen strawberries
1/3 cup frozen raspberries
1/3 cup frozen blueberries
1/3 cup frozen blackberries
1/2 cup milk

DIRECTIONS
Combine all ingredients in the jar of a high-speed blender. Blend until very smooth.

Nutrition per serving:
356 calories, 1g fat, 71g carbs, 21g protein

Under-The-Weather Smoothie

This smoothie is a staple in our house whenever someone is feeling less than stellar. It's packed with immune-boosting vitamin C and a throat-soothing texture.

 1 SERVING **5 MINUTES**

INGREDIENTS
1 cup plain Greek yogurt
1 banana
1 cup frozen peach slices
1 small orange or clementine, peeled
1/2 cup orange juice
A few ice cubes

DIRECTIONS
Combine all ingredients in the jar of a high-speed blender. Blend until very smooth.

Nutrition per serving:
356 calories, 1g fat, 71g carbs, 21g protein

soups

My favorite of all the seasons is summer, but the thought of sipping a steaming bowl of hearty soup by the fireplace is almost enough to get me to change my tune. The winter chill isn't nearly as foreboding when you have a pot of soul-warming deliciousness simmering away on the stove.

Greek yogurt has a lot of incredible uses, but its role as a thickener for hearty, creamy soups is one of my favorites. Chowders and bisques that used to be considered a special-occasion-only kind of treat thanks to high calories and fat are now light enough to be enjoyed every day without sacrificing a drop of flavor.

Soups are also one of my favorite freezer cooking dishes (all the recipes in this section have been freezer-tested). I've been known to double or triple a favorite soup recipe, freeze the extra servings flat in freezer bags, and then reheat in the slow cooker at a later date. Served with some warm, crusty bread, winter dinner doesn't get much easier than that.

velvety POTATO SOUP

When the temps dip down and the leaves start to turn, nothing makes me happier than settling in with a big, steaming bowl of potato soup. Instead of using heavy cream, my lighter version is thickened with light Greek yogurt. All the taste without any guilt!

8 SERVINGS   **45 MINUTES**

INGREDIENTS

2 slices bacon

1 tablespoon butter

Pinch of red pepper flakes

2 cloves garlic, minced

2 medium onions, diced

3 stalks celery, diced

3 pounds potatoes, peeled and diced (about 6 medium potatoes)

6 cups chicken or vegetable stock

1 1/2 cups skim milk

2 bay leaves

1/2 teaspoon dried thyme

Salt and pepper, to taste

1 cup low-fat Greek yogurt

Cheddar cheese, sliced green onions, etc., for topping

DIRECTIONS

In a Dutch oven or soup pot, cook the bacon over medium heat, flipping frequently, until brown and cooked through. Remove from pan, crumble, and set aside. Add butter to the bacon grease in the pot. When melted, add in the red pepper flakes and garlic. Cook until garlic is fragrant, about 3 minutes. Then add the onions and celery. Cook until all vegetables are tender, about 7 minutes. Add in potatoes, stock, milk, bay leaves, thyme, salt, and pepper. Bring to a boil, reduce heat, and simmer for about 30 minutes, or until potatoes are fork-tender. Remove soup from heat, discard bay leaves, and either using an immersion blender or blending in batches in a standard blender, puree until very smooth. If you prefer a chunkier potato soup, you can also use a potato masher to only mash up a few potatoes, or only puree half of the mixture. Once the soup is pureed, stir in the yogurt until well incorporated. Spoon into bowls and top with bacon crumbles plus other desired toppings.

Nutrition per serving:
230 calories, 5g fat, 38g carbs, 7g protein

When the grocery fund is looking a little sad, **this is one of my go-to dishes. Potato-based dishes are a great way to get a large, filling meal without spending a lot of cash on ingredients.**

When butternut squash is in season and the prices plummet in the fall, stock up! In a cool, dark place, unblemished butternut squashes can store for many months—we just keep ours stashed on shelves in the basement.

butternut and APPLE BISQUE

The flavor star of this vegetarian soup is the butternut squash, but the addition of tart apples lends a nice, naturally sweet note that partners beautifully with the warmth of the squash.

 6 SERVINGS   **30 MINUTES**

INGREDIENTS

2 tablespoons olive oil

3 cloves garlic, minced

1 large onion, diced

1 tablespoon peeled and grated fresh ginger

2 large carrots, peeled and chopped

1 large apple, peeled, cored, and chopped

1/4 teaspoon ground cinnamon

2 medium butternut squashes, peeled, seeded, chopped

3 1/2 cups vegetable stock

Salt and pepper, to taste

1/2 cup plain Greek yogurt

DIRECTIONS

Heat olive oil in a large soup pot over medium-low heat. Add garlic, onion, ginger, and carrots, and cook until softened, about 8 minutes. Add in all remaining ingredients except the yogurt. Bring to a boil, reduce heat, and simmer for 25 to 30 minutes, or until all vegetables are very soft. Remove from heat, and puree in batches in a blender or using an immersion blender. Stir in the yogurt. Test for seasoning and add more salt and pepper if necessary.

Nutrition per serving: *176 calories, 6g fat, 28g carbs, 6g protein*

roasted pepper and
WHITE BEAN SOUP

This vegetarian soup falls somewhere between a soup and a pasta dish. If I were you, I'd eat it with a spoon but have a big hunk of crusty bread nearby to sop up all the delicious, creamy stock left behind.

 8 SERVINGS 45 MINUTES

INGREDIENTS

3 large red bell peppers, halved and seeded

2 cups hot water

1 cup sun-dried tomatoes

2 tablespoons olive oil

4 cloves garlic, minced

1 tablespoon minced fresh thyme

1 tablespoon minced fresh oregano

1 (15 ounce) can Great Northern
  beans, drained and rinsed

4 cups vegetable stock

2 cups whole wheat elbow macaroni

1/3 cup plain Greek yogurt

Salt and pepper, to taste

DIRECTIONS

Preheat the broiler. Arrange peppers, skin side up, on a baking sheet and place under broiler. Broil until skins are almost entirely black, flip peppers, and continue to broil for another 5 minutes, or until the peppers are very soft. Remove from broiler and let peppers rest until cool enough to handle. Once cool, peel and chop roughly. Set aside.

Meanwhile, pour the hot water over the sun-dried tomatoes in a large bowl, and let sit for 10 minutes, or until the tomatoes soften. Set aside.

In a large Dutch oven or soup pot, heat the olive oil over medium-high heat. Add in the garlic, and cook until tender and fragrant, about 3 minutes. Add in the thyme and oregano, and cook for an additional minute. Add in the beans, chopped peppers, tomatoes plus liquid, and stock. Bring to a boil, reduce heat, and simmer for 15 minutes. Then add in the elbow macaroni, and cook until macaroni is tender. Remove from heat and let cool for 10 minutes, then add in the yogurt, salt, and pepper.

Nutrition per serving:
233 calories, 7g fat, 35g carbs, 10g protein

creamy
TOMATO-BASIL
bisque

When I was working in the city, there was a lunch spot near my office building that served the best tomato-basil bisque. It was flavorful, creamy, and just a little bit decadent. Because it was tomato-based, I assumed that it was one of the lighter options on the menu, but a quick check of the nutrition facts told a different story. At over 500 calories per small serving, I knew I could do better in my own kitchen. My version is packed with the same flavor, texture, and nutrients, but slashes the calories in half.

YOU'LL NEED

1 tablespoon olive oil

1 tablespoon butter

2 large stalks celery, diced

2 cloves garlic, minced

1 medium onion, diced

3 cups chicken or vegetable stock

6 cups diced tomatoes (about 6 medium tomatoes)

1/2 cup packed basil leaves, chopped

1 tablespoon balsamic vinegar

1/2 cup plain Greek yogurt

Pinch of salt and pepper

4 SERVINGS   20 MINUTES

Nutrition per serving: 231 calories, 4g fat, 14g carbs, 9g protein

1

Heat oil and butter in a soup pot over medium-high heat.

2

Add in the celery, garlic, and onion. Cook until vegetables are tender, about 8 minutes.

3

Add in the stock, tomatoes, and basil.

4

Bring to a boil, reduce heat, and simmer for 10 minutes, or until the tomatoes are beginning to break down.

5

Remove from heat, and puree in batches in a blender or using an immersion blender.

6

Stir in the balsamic vinegar, yogurt, salt, and pepper.

7

Enjoy with a grilled cheese for a classic lunch combo.

SOUPS

cream of...
WHATEVER!
soups

One of the struggles I had when I first made my transition to a whole food, clean diet was the high number of recipes that use "cream of . . ." soups. Condensed soups like these are a great way to add a ton of easy, creamy flavor to casseroles, soups, and other dishes, but healthy eating, they are not. Yes, there are organic and natural versions, but at upward of four dollars a pop (and still packed full of some yucky but "natural" ingredients), I just couldn't justify the cost.

Recently, I've taken to making my own cream of chicken, cream of celery, and cream of mushroom soup for use in recipes. I'll never go back to the can! These recipes are packed with so much more flavor and nutrition than their store-shelf counterparts. Plus, they're a breeze to make!

I like to freeze these soups in 2-cup increments (about the size of the soup can) in small freezer bags. That way I'm always ready if I have a recipe that calls for a condensed soup.

CREAM OF CHICKEN SOUP

 8 CUPS   **30 MINUTES**

INGREDIENTS

1 tablespoon olive oil

1 tablespoon butter

2 cloves garlic, minced

1/2 medium onion, diced

1 pound cooked white-meat chicken, diced

3 cups chicken stock

1 teaspoon dried thyme

1 teaspoon dried sage

1/2 cup plain Greek yogurt

Salt and pepper, to taste

DIRECTIONS

In a soup pot, heat the olive oil and butter over medium-high heat. Add in the garlic and onion, and cook until vegetables are tender, about 8 minutes. Add in the chicken, stock, thyme, and sage. Bring to a boil, reduce heat, and simmer for 10 minutes, or until the onion is very soft. Remove from heat, and puree in batches in a blender or using an immersion blender. Stir in the yogurt, salt, and pepper.

Nutrition per cup: *154 calories, 8g fat, 1g carbs, 18g protein*

Cream of Mushroom Soup

 8 CUPS   **30 MINUTES**

INGREDIENTS

1 tablespoon olive oil

1 tablespoon butter

2 cloves garlic, minced

1/2 medium onion, diced

1 pound button mushrooms, sliced

3 cups chicken or vegetable stock

1 teaspoon dried thyme

1 teaspoon dried sage

1/2 cup plain Greek yogurt

Salt and pepper, to taste

DIRECTIONS

In a soup pot, heat the olive oil and butter over medium-high heat. Add in the garlic, onion, and mushrooms, and cook until vegetables are tender, about 8 minutes. Add in the stock, thyme, and sage. Bring to a boil, reduce heat, and simmer for 10 minutes, or until the mushrooms are very soft. Remove from heat, and puree in batches in a blender or using an immersion blender. Stir in the yogurt, salt, and pepper.

Nutrition per serving: 59 calories, 4g fat, 3g carbs, 4g protein

CREAM OF CELERY SOUP

🥛 8 CUPS   🕐 30 MINUTES

INGREDIENTS

1 tablespoon olive oil

1 tablespoon butter

2 cloves garlic, minced

1/2 medium onion, diced

1 pound celery (stalks and leaves), diced
    (about 16 medium stalks)

3 cups chicken or vegetable stock

1 teaspoon dried thyme

1 teaspoon dried sage

1/2 cup plain Greek yogurt

Salt and pepper, to taste

DIRECTIONS

In a soup pot, heat the olive oil and butter over medium-high heat. Add in the garlic, onion, and celery, and cook until vegetables are tender, about 8 minutes. Add in the stock, thyme, and sage. Bring to a boil, reduce heat, and simmer for 10 minutes, or until the celery is very soft. Remove from heat, and puree in batches in a blender or using an immersion blender. Stir in the yogurt, salt, and pepper.

Nutrition per serving: 56 calories, 4g fat, 3g carbs, 2g protein

roasted corn and
TOMATILLO SOUP

By roasting the corn and tomatillos under the broiler, you get a ton of slow-cooked flavor without spending a lot of time in the kitchen.

 4 SERVINGS   **25 MINUTES**

INGREDIENTS

4 cups frozen corn

16 tomatillos, husks removed

2 tablespoons butter

4 cloves garlic, minced

1 large onion, diced

1 jalapeño, seeded and diced finely

4 cups vegetable or chicken stock

1 tablespoon ground cumin

Salt and pepper, to taste

1/3 cup plain Greek yogurt

Minced cilantro, for garnish

DIRECTIONS

Preheat the broiler. Place the corn and tomatillos on a baking sheet and place under the broiler. Cook for 10 to 15 minutes, flipping halfway through, or until the tomatillos are mostly browned and soft, and the corn has begun to brown. Meanwhile, melt the butter in a soup pot over medium-high heat. Add in the garlic, onion, and jalapeño, and cook until tender, about 5 minutes. Add in the roasted tomatillos, corn, stock, cumin, salt, and pepper. Bring to a boil, reduce heat, and simmer for about 10 minutes, or until tomatillos are very tender. Remove from heat. Using a wooden spoon or a potato masher, smash the tomatillos until no large chunks are left. Stir in the yogurt and serve.

Nutrition per serving: 291 calories, 10g fat, 44g carbs, 13g protein

Tomatillos are available at many major grocery stores (they look like small, hard green tomatoes wrapped in a papery husk). But if you're having a hard time finding them, check your local Mexican grocery store or a farmers' market.

broccoli, cheddar, and POTATO SOUP

This is one of those soups that feels so incredibly decadent and sinful that you'll have a hard time believing it isn't loaded with heavy cream. Using lighter Greek yogurt in place of cream leaves us some room to go heavy-handed with the cheddar cheese. Who doesn't love cheese?

 **6 SERVINGS**    **30 MINUTES**

INGREDIENTS

2 tablespoons butter

1 medium onion, diced

2 medium carrots, peeled and diced

4 medium stalks celery, diced

4 large potatoes, peeled and diced

4 cups broccoli florets

5 cups chicken or vegetable stock

3/4 cup shredded sharp cheddar cheese

1/2 cup plain Greek yogurt

Salt and pepper, to taste

DIRECTIONS

In a soup pot, melt the butter over medium-high heat. Add in the onions, carrots, and celery, and cook until vegetables are tender, about 12 minutes. Add in the potatoes, broccoli, and stock. Bring to a boil, reduce heat, and simmer until the potatoes and broccoli are both tender, about 15 minutes. Remove from heat, and puree in batches in a blender or using an immersion blender. Stir in the cheddar cheese until melted. Then stir in the yogurt, salt, and pepper.

Nutrition per serving: *341 calories, 10g fat, 48g carbs, 15g protein*

wedding
CAULIFLOWER SOUP

When someone says "cauliflower soup," it probably sounds like something an evil lunch lady would serve to school kids as a torture device. But a well-executed cauliflower soup is smooth, comforting, and incredibly elegant.

My foodie sister-in-law served cauliflower soup at her wedding reception, and it was hands down one of the best soups I've ever eaten—wedding or not. It was so delicious that I hurried home after the wedding and whipped up my own version. Six years later, it's still in heavy rotation in our house.

 4 SERVINGS **30 MINUTES**

INGREDIENTS

1 tablespoon olive oil
1 tablespoon butter
1 medium onion, diced
1 medium carrot, peeled and diced
1 medium stalk celery, diced
1 clove garlic, minced
4 tablespoons minced fresh parsley
1 head cauliflower, leaves and core
    removed, roughly chopped
4 cups chicken or vegetable stock
1 cup plain Greek yogurt
Salt and pepper, to taste

DIRECTIONS

Heat olive oil and butter in a Dutch oven or soup pot over medium-low heat. Cook onion, carrots, celery, and garlic until just slightly tender, about 10 minutes. Stir in parsley and cauliflower. Cover and let steam for 10 minutes. Uncover, add stock, bring to a boil, and simmer for another 10 to 15 minutes, or until all vegetables are very tender (think mushy). Remove from heat, and puree in batches in a blender or using an immersion blender. Stir in the yogurt, salt, and pepper.

Nutrition per serving:
127 calories, 4g fat, 11g carbs, 11g protein

For the smoothest cauliflower soup, make sure you really cook the cauliflower until it's fall-apart soft, and usethe highest setting on your blender.

cool CUCUMBER SOUP

You may be skeptical of a cold soup (especially one packed with cucumbers), but this soup is surprisingly flavorful and incredibly refreshing. I love serving it next to Lamb Koftas (page 105) because the light flavor of the soup is such a great balance with the richness of the meat. Yum!

 6 SERVINGS   **10 MINUTES (PLUS CHILLING TIME)**

INGREDIENTS

3 medium cucumbers, peeled, seeded, and chopped

1 yellow bell pepper, seeded and chopped

3 green onions, sliced light-green and white parts only

1 tablespoon fresh mint leaves

1 tablespoon fresh oregano leaves

1 tablespoon minced fresh chives

Pinch of ground cayenne

2 clove garlic, smashed

1/2 teaspoon salt, plus more to taste

3 cups plain Greek yogurt

2 tablespoons olive oil

1 tablespoon white wine vinegar

1/4 cup milk

DIRECTIONS

Combine all the ingredients in the jar of a blender, or in a large bowl if using an immersion blender. Blend on high until very smooth. Taste for seasoning, adjusting if necessary. Refrigerate for at least 2 hours to allow flavors to meld.

Nutrition per serving: 130 calories, 5g fat, 12g carbs, 11g protein

If you're serving this for a crowd, make sure to put out some hot sauce for those folks who like it a little bit hotter.

low country SEAFOOD CHOWDER

This cozy, creamy soup combines two of my favorite foods—a Low Country boil and corn chowder. This recipe is completely customizable. Not a shrimp fan? Leave it out. Love lobster? Add lots!

 8 SERVINGS    50 MINUTES

INGREDIENTS

2 slices thick-cut bacon

1/4 teaspoon red pepper flakes

2 cloves garlic, minced

1 medium onion, diced

1 1/2 pounds new potatoes, diced

4 cups fish or vegetable stock

1 teaspoon seafood seasoning
   (such as Old Bay Seasoning)

2 bay leaves

1/2 teaspoon celery seed

1 cup frozen corn kernels

12 ounces Andouille sausage, sliced into coins

1 1/2 pounds assorted raw seafood
   (shrimp, mussels, calamari, lobster, firm
   whitefish, clams, crabs, etc.)

2/3 cup plain Greek yogurt

DIRECTIONS

In a large Dutch oven or stock pot, cook bacon over medium heat until crisp. Remove bacon, drain on paper towels, and crumble, then set aside. Reduce heat on stock pot to low, add in red pepper flakes and garlic, and cook until fragrant, about 2 minutes. Add in the onion and cook until soft, about 5 minutes. Add potatoes, stock, seafood seasoning, bay leaves, celery seed, frozen corn, and sausage. Turn heat to high and bring to a boil. Then reduce heat and simmer for 30 to 40 minutes, or until potatoes are tender. Add in the seafood and cook for 4 to 5 minutes, or until the seafood is opaque and cooked through. Remove pot from heat and discard bay leaves. Let soup cool for 5 minutes. Then stir in yogurt. Spoon into bowls and serve with crumbled bacon on top.

Nutrition per serving: *341 calories, 10g fat, 48g carbs, 15g protein*

sweet corn CHOWDER

There aren't a lot of soups that I'll serve in the middle of summer heat, but this corn chowder is light and sweet enough to stand up to even the hottest July day. This soup showcases the very best of summertime—ripe sweet corn.

 **4 SERVINGS**   **50 MINUTES**

INGREDIENTS

4 ears sweet corn,
   husks removed
2 tablespoons butter
1 large onion, diced
1 large carrot, peeled and diced
1 medium stalk celery, diced
1 clove garlic, minced
4 cups vegetable stock

2 medium potatoes,
   peeled and diced
1 red bell pepper,
   seeded and diced
2 bay leaves
1/2 teaspoon dried thyme
1 cup plain Greek yogurt
Salt and pepper, to taste

DIRECTIONS

To remove corn kernels from cobs: Place a small bowl upside down inside a large bowl. Rest the end of the ear of corn on the small bowl and use a sharp knife to slice off the kernels into the large bowl. Reserve the corn cob. Repeat with remaining ears of corn. Set aside. In a Dutch oven or soup pot, melt the butter over medium-high heat. Add in the onion, carrot, celery, and garlic, and cook until tender, about 10 minutes. Add in the corn kernels, corn cobs, vegetable stock, potatoes, bell pepper, bay leaves, and thyme. Bring to a boil, reduce heat, and simmer until the vegetables are very tender, about 30 minutes. Remove from heat. Discard the bay leaves and corn cobs. Let soup cool for 10 minutes, then stir in the yogurt, salt, and pepper.

Nutrition per serving:
283 calories, 8g fat, 41g carbs, 14g protein

To get the most corn flavor per bite, this recipe uses the corn two ways—the fresh, plump kernels, and the cobs simmered in the stock.

INGREDIENTS

2 slices thick-cut bacon, diced
2 tablespoons butter
4 cloves garlic, minced
1 large onion, diced
1 jalapeño, seeded, diced
3 cups chicken stock
1 tablespoon Worcestershire sauce

1 tablespoon ground cumin
3 (14 ounce) cans black beans,
   drained and rinsed
1 (28 ounce) can diced tomatoes
1 tablespoon dried oregano
1 (12 ounce) can beer
   (your favorite)

1 bunch cilantro, chopped
Juice and zest of 1 lime
Salt and pepper, to taste
Greek yogurt, shredded cheese,
   diced avocado, for topping

DIRECTIONS

In a Dutch oven or soup pot over medium-high heat, cook the bacon until some of the fat has released, about 2 minutes. Add in the garlic, onion, and jalapeño, and cook until fragrant and tender, about 5 minutes. Add in the stock, Worcestershire sauce, cumin, beans, diced tomatoes, oregano, and beer. Bring to a boil, reduce heat, and simmer for 30 minutes, or until thick and bubbly. Remove from heat and stir in the cilantro, lime juice and zest, salt, and pepper. Serve with a big dollop of Greek yogurt and other favorite toppings.

SOUPS

80   ***Nutrition per serving:*** *537 calories, 7g fat, 86g carbs, 31g protein*

If you like a thicker, stick-to-your-ribs kind of chili, just drop the amount of chicken stock in the recipe down to 2 cups.

mains

*T*t may seem like a stretch to use Greek yogurt as a central ingredient in entrées, but I've found that it works incredibly well to add creaminess, thickness, and tangy flavor to a lot of our favorite dinnertime dishes.

Since Greek yogurt is such a versatile substitute in the kitchen (see Simple Substitutions, page 22), you can use it in almost any dish calling for cream cheese, heavy cream, sour cream, or mayo. That's a lot of future dinners that are Greek yogurt–friendly!

If you're a vegetarian, using Greek yogurt in your dinners is an efficient way to add lean, meatless protein to your diet. And if you're a meat-eater, you'll love the creamy quality that Greek yogurt adds to sauces, casseroles, and pasta dishes. In these pages you'll find a mix of recipes that will satisfy both meat-lovers and veg-heads.

steak salad with
BLUE CHEESE DRESSING

I'm not much of a salad person. And while you'll never catch me ordering a salad at a restaurant, there are a few made-at-home salads that make even my salad-hating heart sing. This is one of them! It's a light dinner that feels satisfying thanks to the combination of steak, walnuts, and a creamy (without the cream) blue cheese dressing.

 4 DINNER-SIZED SALADS   **10 MINUTES**

INGREDIENTS

1 cup plain Greek yogurt
2 tablespoons minced fresh chives
1/2 cup crumbled blue cheese
1/4 cup diced onion
Salt and pepper, to taste
1/2 cup milk
2 teaspoons lemon juice

2 heads romaine, washed and cut into
 bite-size pieces
1 large red onion, sliced
1 cup cherry tomatoes, halved
1 pound sirloin steak, grilled, chilled,
 and sliced thinly
1/2 cup chopped walnuts, toasted

DIRECTIONS

In a small bowl, whisk together the yogurt, chives, blue cheese, onion, salt, pepper, milk, and lemon juice. Set aside. To assemble salads, divide romaine onto four plates, and top with red onion, cherry tomatoes, steak, and walnuts. Drizzle dressing over entire salad.

MAINS

Nutrition per serving: 484 calories, 23g fat, 21g carbs, 52g protein

We use this blue cheese dressing on just about everything! It's particularly delicious as a dipping sauce for hot wings.

For a vegetarian version of this, leave out the tuna, and add a second can of chickpeas and a splash of soy sauce.

creamy chickpea and
TUNA SALAD

Everyone seems to have their own twist on classic tuna salad. I like making a version that is light on the tuna and mayo, and heavy on the vegetables. This salad works well in a sandwich or with crackers, but I love piling it onto a fresh bed of greens for a really healthy lunch.

 4 SERVINGS   **10 MINUTES**

INGREDIENTS

1 (14 ounce) can chickpeas, drained and rinsed
2 (5 ounce) cans chunk light tuna, packed in water, drained
2 tablespoons mayonnaise
1/2 cup plain Greek yogurt
1 tablespoon Dijon mustard
2 medium stalks celery, diced
1/2 medium onion, diced
1 teaspoon minced fresh dill
1/4 cup unsalted sunflower seeds
Salt and pepper, to taste

DIRECTIONS

Combine all the ingredients in a large bowl. Serve immediately, or refrigerate for a few hours to allow the flavors to meld.

Nutrition per serving: 230 calories, 11g fat, 9g carbs, 24g protein

LEMON CREAM

This brightly flavored pasta dish feels too simple to be anything spectacular. You might even find yourself fighting the urge to add a dash of this and a dash of that, but I promise your restraint will pay off. The simple flavors of this dish are what make it so special. Enjoy the simplicity!

 6 SERVINGS   **20 MINUTES**

INGREDIENTS

1 pound angel hair pasta

1 tablespoon butter

1 clove garlic, minced

1/3 cup minced fresh parsley

1/3 cup minced fresh oregano

1/4 cup minced fresh chives

1 cup chicken or vegetable stock

Juice and zest of 1 lemon

1/2 cup plain Greek yogurt

1/2 cup shredded Parmesan cheese

DIRECTIONS

Cook angel hair in salted water according to package directions. Reserve about 1 cup of pasta cooking water. Drain pasta and set aside. Meanwhile, melt the butter in a small saucepan over medium heat. Add in the garlic, parsley, oregano, and chives, and cook until the garlic is tender and fragrant, about 3 minutes. Remove from heat, stir in the chicken or vegetable stock, lemon zest and juice, and yogurt. Pour sauce over hot angel hair and toss to coat, using some of the reserved pasta cooking water, if needed, to thin out the sauce. Serve topped with Parmesan.

MAINS

Nutrition per serving: 323 calories, 8g fat, 47g carbs, 17g protein

Shrimp and chicken are both excellent lean proteins to add to this pasta. Just add into the saucepan when you add the herbs, and sauté until cooked.

asparagus and SWISS QUICHE

Quiche is a dish that seems really fussy and fancy, but actually comes without a whole lot of work. Many quiche recipes call for a decent dose of heavy cream, but here we're subbing in Greek yogurt. Not only does it lighten the entire dish, but it also adds a nice tangy flavor that balances with the richness of the Swiss cheese.

8 SERVINGS   1 HOUR 15 MINUTES

INGREDIENTS

Prepared pie crust
1/2 pound fresh asparagus, woody stems trimmed
2 tablespoons butter
1/2 large onion, diced
1 clove garlic, minced
6 eggs
1 1/2 cups plain Greek yogurt
1 teaspoon salt
1 teaspoon pepper
1/3 cup shredded Swiss cheese

DIRECTIONS

Preheat oven to 325°. Press prepared pie crust into a 9-inch pie plate, flute edges, and set aside. Reserve 3 thin spears of asparagus for garnish, then cut the remaining asparagus into 1-inch pieces. Melt the butter in a large skillet over medium-high heat. Add in the onion and garlic, and cook until translucent and fragrant, about 3 minutes. Add in the asparagus and continue cooking until asparagus is bright green and softened, about 5 minutes. Remove from heat and spoon into the prepared pie crust.

In a mixing bowl, whisk together the eggs, yogurt, salt, and pepper. Pour over the asparagus mixture. Sprinkle the cheese on top. Bake for 10 minutes, then remove and arrange reserved asparagus spears on top for garnish. Continue to bake for another 35 to 40 minutes, or until the quiche is set. Let rest for 10 minutes before slicing.

Nutrition per serving:
200 calories, 13g fat, 12g carbs, 10g protein

This quiche freezes and reheats well.

Just bake the quiche in an aluminum pie pan, and then once it has completely cooled, wrap tightly in plastic wrap. To defrost, set in the fridge overnight, and then bake in a 350° oven for 15 to 20 minutes, or until warm through.

Don't worry, the mixture will be soupy when you pour it into the baking dish. In the oven, the macaroni will soak up the sauce like a sponge, and the squash will thicken.

beer and butternut squash
MAC AND CHEESE

The inspiration for this fun twist on mac and cheese comes from my love of local beer. The cheese sauce combines Greek yogurt with wheat beer, butternut squash, and a mixture of two cheeses to get an incredibly unique dish.

 **8 SERVINGS**   **1 HOUR**

INGREDIENTS

1 (12 ounce) package whole wheat elbow macaroni

1 small butternut squash (about 1 pound), peeled, seeded, and cubed

3/4 cup wheat beer

1 clove garlic, smashed and peeled

1 bay leaf

Salt and pepper, to taste

1 cup skim milk

1/2 cup plain Greek yogurt

3/4 cup shredded Gruyère cheese

1/2 cup shredded Romano cheese

1 tablespoon butter

2 tablespoons panko bread crumbs

DIRECTIONS

Preheat oven to 375°. Prepare a 9 x 9-inch baking dish by spraying it liberally with cooking spray. Cook elbow macaroni according to package directions, omitting fat and salt. Drain and set aside. In a large saucepan, combine squash, beer, garlic, bay leaf, salt, pepper, and milk. Bring to a boil, reduce heat, and simmer until squash is very tender, about 25 minutes. The mixture may begin to separate; this is fine. Remove from heat and discard bay leaf. Using an immersion blender, or a standard blender with the steam vent removed, blend squash mixture together until very smooth and creamy. Pour mixture into a large mixing bowl and stir in yogurt, Gruyère, Romano, and butter until cheeses are melted. Add in elbow macaroni and stir until well coated. Pour the mixture into the prepared baking dish. Sprinkle bread crumbs evenly over top. Bake for 30 minutes, or until top is browned and crunchy, and sauce is thickened.

Nutrition per serving: *245 calories, 13g fat, 17g carbs, 15g protein*

gyro NACHOS

I grew up in a tiny rural town, so my exposure to international foods was admittedly low. But once I moved away to college in the big city, I fell head over heels in love with exploring international cuisine. One of my favorite Middle Eastern restaurants had the incredible idea of making this gyro and nacho fusion, and I've been making my own version ever since I first ordered it. The highlight of these nachos is the Greek yogurt–based tzatziki sauce. It's so flavorful and light, you'll want to use it on everything!

YOU'LL NEED

1/2 large cucumber, peeled and diced

1 cup plain Greek yogurt

1 clove garlic, minced

1 tablespoon minced dill (fresh or dried)

1 tablespoon lemon juice

Salt and pepper to taste

4 whole wheat pitas

1 pound ground lamb

1 tablespoon Greek seasoning (such as Cavender's)

1 tablespoon dried oregano

Your favorite gyro toppings, such as chopped cucumber, chopped tomatoes, crumbled feta, sliced black olives, chopped parsley, diced red onion, etc.

Nutrition per serving: : 213 calories, 5g fat, 20g carbs, 22g protein (does not include extra toppings)

1 For tzatziki sauce: In a small mixing bowl, combine the cucumber, yogurt, garlic, dill, lemon juice, salt, and pepper. Set aside.

2 Preheat the oven to 425°.

3 Pull apart the two sides of each pita (so they are only "one-ply"), and using a pizza cutter, slice each into eight triangles.

4 Arrange in one layer on a baking sheet, spray with cooking spray, and bake for 10 to 12 minutes, or until crispy and brown.

5 Meanwhile, in a large skillet, brown the lamb with the Greek seasoning and oregano over medium-low heat until cooked through. Remove from skillet and drain on paper towels. Set aside.

6 To assemble nachos, layer pita chips on a plate, and top with lamb, prepared tzatziki, and favorite toppings.

green chicken ENCHILADAS

Enchiladas definitely hold a spot on my list of comfort foods. This version has all the comfort of the typical flavorful, filling, and gooey cheese, but in a much lighter and healthier recipe.

6 SERVINGS   1 HOUR

INGREDIENTS

12 medium corn tortillas

2 tablespoons coconut oil

4 cloves garlic, minced

1 large onion, diced

1 jalapeño, seeded, minced

2 teaspoons ground cumin

1 teaspoon salt

1/2 teaspoon black pepper

1 1/2 cups shredded cooked
  chicken breast

1/4 cup chopped cilantro

3/4 cup plus 1/4 cup shredded
  Monterey Jack cheese

1/2 cup plain Greek yogurt

Juice and zest of one lime

2 (10 ounce) cans green
  enchilada sauce
  (found in the international
  foods aisle)

DIRECTIONS

Preheat oven to 350°. Wrap tortillas in aluminum foil and let warm in oven while it preheats. Meanwhile, melt the coconut oil over medium-high heat in a large skillet. Add in the garlic, onion, jalapeño, cumin, salt, pepper, and chicken. Cook until the vegetables are tender and fragrant, about 5 minutes. Remove from heat, and transfer mixture to a heatproof mixing bowl. Add in the cilantro, 3/4 cup of cheese, yogurt, lime juice, and lime zest. Stir until well mixed.

To assemble enchiladas, pour a small amount of green enchilada sauce into the bottom of a 9 x 13-inch casserole dish. Remove tortillas from oven, and fill with about 1/3 cup of the chicken mixture. Roll tortilla tight, and place in the casserole, seam side down. Repeat with remaining tortillas and filling. When all tortillas are filled, pour remaining enchilada sauce over top, and sprinkle with remaining cheese. Bake for 25 to 30 minutes, or until browned and bubbly.

Nutrition per serving:
305 calories, 13g fat, 26g carbs, 22g protein

While this is far from a traditional dish, **traditional enchiladas do use corn tortillas for good reason—they hold up well to cooking and retain their chew.**

top it OFF

Greek yogurt can help you expand way past the usual set of condiments. Ketchup, mustard, and mayo aren't the only way to add a ton of flavor to sandwiches, burgers, and fries. These are three of my favorite Greek yogurt–based condiments, but the possibilities are pretty much limitless. Grab a tub of yogurt and get to experimenting!

Sriracha Spiced Yogurt

This spicy, tangy condiment is my favorite! I put it on almost everything—burgers, vegetables, sandwiches. This sauce is incredible on Spicy Black Bean Sliders (page 102). The best part about this sauce is you have complete control over the spice. The amounts below create a medium-spicy condiment.

 ABOUT 1/3 CUP   **5 MINUTES**

INGREDIENTS
1/4 cup plain Greek yogurt
1 tablespoon Dijon mustard
2 tablespoons hot pepper sauce (I like the sriracha variety)
1 tablespoon mayonnaise
Salt and pepper, to taste

DIRECTIONS
Whisk all the ingredients together in a small bowl. Taste and adjust seasonings, if necessary.

Nutrition per cup: 154 calories, 8g fat, 1g carbs, 18g protein

Honey Mustard Yogurt

This sweet and tangy dressing is my husband's favorite. It has the consistency of a dip, so he likes to use it with pizza crusts, vegetables, and chips. You can also thin it out with a bit more vinegar for a tangy salad dressing.

 ABOUT 1/2 CUP   **5 MINUTES**

INGREDIENTS

1/2 cup plain Greek yogurt
2 tablespoons honey
2 tablespoons Dijon mustard

Pinch of salt
1 tablespoon apple cider vinegar
1 tablespoon mayonnaise

DIRECTIONS

Whisk all the ingredients together in a small bowl. Taste and adjust seasonings, if necessary.

Nutrition per cup: 154 calories, 8g fat, 1g carbs, 18g protein

Yogurt Ranch Dressing

We're a little bit obsessed with ranch dressing in my house. But the stuff that comes in the bottle? No, thank you. It's packed full of chemicals and artificial flavors. This lighter version is just as flavorful without the questionable ingredients. For a thicker dip version, just leave out the milk and sub in more Greek yogurt.

 ABOUT 1/2 CUP   **5 MINUTES**

INGREDIENTS

1/3 cup plain Greek yogurt
1/4 cup milk
1 tablespoon white vinegar
1/2 teaspoon dried chives
1/2 teaspoon dried parsley
1/2 teaspoon dried dill

1 tablespoon mayonnaise
1/2 teaspoon garlic powder
1/2 teaspoon onion powder
1/4 teaspoon salt
1/4 teaspoon pepper

DIRECTIONS

Whisk all the ingredients together in a small bowl. Taste and adjust seasonings, if necessary.

Nutrition per cup: 154 calories, 8g fat, 1g carbs, 18g protein

While grilling these burgers adds a great smoky flavor, you can easily prepare them in the oven, too. Just preheat to 425° and cook on a baking sheet for about 12 minutes (for a well-done burger), flipping halfway through.

maple-bacon burgers with
SWEET DIJON SAUCE

These burgers are delicious, but a little on the decadent side. We save them for special occasions. In fact, my husband requests these burgers for his birthday every year. The sweet, creamy sauce balances out the richness of the burger patty and the saltiness of the bacon. It's a winner.

 4 BURGERS   **20 MINUTES**

INGREDIENTS

1 tablespoon Dijon mustard
2 tablespoons maple syrup
1/4 cup plain Greek yogurt
1 tablespoon mayonnaise
1 pound lean ground beef
1/2 cup unsweetened applesauce
1 teaspoon salt

1 teaspoon pepper
1 cup bread crumbs
4 whole-grain hamburger buns
4 slices thick-cut bacon, cooked
Hamburger fixings
    (tomatoes, lettuce, onions, etc.)

DIRECTIONS

In a small bowl, whisk together the mustard, maple syrup, yogurt, and mayo. Let chill in the fridge while you make the burgers. Preheat grill. Combine beef, applesauce, salt, pepper, and 1/2 cup of the bread crumbs in a large bowl, adding more bread crumbs if the mixture feels too soft. Form into four patties and grill on both sides until desired doneness is reached. To assemble burgers, place patty on a bun and top with desired fixings, a slice of bacon, and a large dollop of the sauce.

Nutrition per serving: 509 calories, 16g fat, 45g carbs, 45g protein

spicy BLACK BEAN SLIDERS

I'm not a vegetarian, but I love vegetarian food, and these black bean burgers are one of my very favorite meatless meals. I like to make these into sliders because, let's be honest, everything tastes better when it's miniaturized, right?

 12 SLIDERS   **30 MINUTES**

INGREDIENTS

Cooking spray

1 (15 ounce) can black beans, drained and rinsed

1 medium green bell pepper, roughly chopped

1/2 medium onion, roughly chopped

3 cloves garlic

1 egg

1 tablespoon chili powder

Salt and pepper, to taste

1 teaspoon hot pepper sauce

2 cups bread crumbs

12 lettuce leaves

12 red onion slices

12 whole wheat slider buns

1 batch of Sriracha Spiced Yogurt (page 98)

DIRECTIONS

Preheat oven to 350°. Spray a baking sheet with cooking spray and set aside. In the basin of a food processor, pulse together the black beans, green pepper, onion, garlic, egg, chili powder, salt, pepper, and hot pepper sauce until well mixed. The mixture will be pretty liquid. Transfer the black bean mixture into a medium mixing bowl, and stir in the bread crumbs. Form mixture into 12 slider-sized patties and place on prepared baking sheet. Bake for 20 minutes, flipping once halfway through baking, or until the burgers have begun to dry out and turn golden brown. To assemble sliders, place a leaf of lettuce, one slider patty, some red onion rings, and a dollop of the sauce onto each slider bun.

MAINS

Nutrition per slider: 221 calories, 4g fat, 37g carbs, 11g protein

These burgers are great freezer food. Just let them cool completely after baking, then stash in a zip-top freezer bag. A few seconds in the microwave or a quick trip on the grill, and you have a veggie burger.

I love the flavor of lamb in these meatballs, but you can easily sub in lean ground beef if that's all you have on hand.

lamb koftas with YOGURT-MINT SAUCE

These little spiced Middle Eastern meatballs pack so much interesting flavor—especially when paired with the cool, creamy dipping sauce. I love serving these with warm pita bread as a special dinner, but they also work well as a fun international appetizer for gatherings.

 6 SERVINGS   **30 MINUTES**

INGREDIENTS

Dipping sauce

2 green onions, sliced, green and white parts only

1/4 cup packed mint leaves, chopped

1/4 cup packed oregano leaves, chopped

2 tablespoons fresh dill

1 tablespoon olive oil

1 tablespoon lemon juice

1 cup plain Greek yogurt

Salt and pepper, to taste

Koftas

1 pound ground lamb

4 cloves garlic, minced finely

1 teaspoon salt

3 green onions, sliced, green and white parts only

3 tablespoons minced fresh parsley

1 tablespoon ground coriander

2 tablespoons ground cumin

2 tablespoons fresh oregano

Pinch of ground cinnamon

Pinch of black pepper

DIRECTIONS

Preheat oven to 375°. Add all the sauce ingredients in the basin of a food processor, and pulse until herbs are minced finely and the mixture is well combined. Transfer to a serving bowl and stash in the fridge while you prepare the koftas.

In a large mixing bowl, combine all the kofta ingredients, mixing well with clean hands. Form mixture into 1-inch balls (you should get about 18). Place koftas on a baking sheet, 1 inch apart, and bake for 10 to 12 minutes, flipping halfway through.

Nutrition per serving: 206 calories, 9g fat, 6g carbs, 26g protein

12 ounces whole wheat penne

1 tablespoon
olive oil

4 cloves garlic,
minced

Pinch each of red
pepper flakes,
pepper, and salt

8 ounces button
mushrooms, sliced

2 medium tomatoes (about
1/2 pound), chopped

4 cups fresh spinach

10 ounces medium raw
shrimp, peeled and deveined

1/2 cup
marinara sauce

1/3 cup plain
Greek yogurt

1/4 cup shredded
Parmesan cheese

SPICY PENNE
with shrimp

If you show up any given weekday evening at our house, you have a pretty good chance of stumbling on us eating this pasta dish for dinner. It's in our regular menu rotation because it is so simple, so nutritious, and so flavorful.

Nutrition per serving: 364 calories, 9g fat, 48g carbs, 28g protein

1

Cook penne according to package directions, omitting salt and fat. Drain and set aside.

2

In a large skillet with a lid, heat olive oil over medium-low heat. Add in garlic, red pepper flakes, pepper, and salt, and cook for 2 minutes, or until garlic begins to soften.

3

Add in mushrooms and tomatoes. Cook for 5 minutes, or until mushrooms begin to release their water.

4

Add in the spinach, cover skillet, and let spinach wilt for about 2 minutes.

5

Turn heat up to medium-high and add in shrimp. Cook for 1 to 2 minutes, or until shrimp are pink and opaque.

6

Add in the marinara sauce and stir until all items are well-coated. Continue cooking until heated through, about 2 minutes.

7

Remove pan from heat, wait 5 minutes, and then stir in the yogurt.

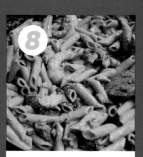

8

Add in the cooked penne and toss to coat. Serve topped with Parmesan cheese.

creamy chicken and
KALE ALFREDO

I think the green, earthy kale in this Alfredo dish is a really nice balance to the richness of the cheesy, creamy sauce. Plus, you get your salad and pasta all in one bowl! I love that even steamed kale retains some of its chew, but if you aren't a fan, you can easily sub in baby spinach for a less chewy but equally healthy option.

 6 SERVINGS   **45 MINUTES**

INGREDIENTS

13 ounces whole wheat fettuccine

1 bunch kale, stems removed and torn into bite-size pieces

1 tablespoon butter

1 tablespoon olive oil

2 cloves garlic, minced

1 cup chicken stock

1/2 cup water

1 tablespoon cornstarch

1/2 cup shredded Parmesan cheese

1/2 cup plain Greek yogurt

Salt and pepper, to taste

2 cups chopped cooked chicken

DIRECTIONS

Cook pasta according to package directions. Before draining, line a colander with the kale. Reserving about 1/2 cup of the pasta cooking water, drain pasta over the kale and return both the kale and pasta to cooking pot. The steam from the pasta will continue to wilt the kale. Set aside. While pasta is cooking, melt butter and olive oil in a medium saucepan over medium heat. Add in minced garlic and cook until tender and fragrant, about 4 minutes. Add in chicken stock, and bring to a boil. In a small bowl, whisk together the water and cornstarch. Add mixture to the chicken stock, reduce heat, and simmer for 5 to 7 minutes, or until the sauce is thickened. Turn off heat, slide pot over to a cool burner, and whisk in the shredded Parmesan cheese until melted. Let rest 5 minutes, then whisk in the yogurt. Season with salt and pepper. Pour sauce into the pot with the pasta and kale, and toss to coat, adding in some of the reserved pasta water if the mixture is too dry. Divide pasta onto plates and top with chopped chicken and shredded Parmesan.

Nutrition per serving:
421 calories, 12g fat, 49g carbs, 30g protein

This Alfredo sauce is a versatile, healthier version of the classic.
We use it as pizza sauce and a dipping sauce for bread sticks, too.

If you want to save a few minutes, jarred roasted red peppers are a great option. You can usually find them in the condiment aisle of your grocery store, near the olives.

roasted red pepper
SPAGHETTI

Just the incredible smell of red peppers roasting in the oven is enough to make this recipe worth your time. Thankfully, this dish not only smells amazing but tastes it, too. You might not ever go back to regular tomato sauce for spaghetti night.

 **4 SERVINGS**   **30 MINUTES**

INGREDIENTS

4 red bell peppers, halved and seeded

13 ounces whole wheat spaghetti

2 tablespoons butter

1 large onion, diced

3 cloves garlic, minced

1 cup chicken or vegetable stock

1/2 teaspoon salt

1/2 teaspoon pepper

1/3 cup dry red wine

1/2 cup plain Greek yogurt

1/2 cup shredded Parmesan

1/4 cup chopped fresh parsley

DIRECTIONS

Preheat the broiler. Arrange peppers, skin side up, on a baking sheet and place under broiler. Broil until skins are almost entirely black, flip peppers, and continue to broil for another 5 minutes, or until the peppers are very soft. Remove from broiler and let peppers rest until cool enough to handle. Once cool, peel and chop roughly. Set aside. Cook the spaghetti according to package directions, drain, and set aside. In a large skillet, melt the butter over medium-high heat. Add in the onion and garlic, and cook until translucent and fragrant, about 5 minutes. Add in the roasted red peppers, stock, salt, pepper, and wine. Bring to a boil, reduce heat, and simmer for 5 minutes, or until the sauce is thickened. Remove from heat and either using an immersion blender, or blending in batches in a standard blender, puree until smooth. Stir in the yogurt, Parmesan, and parsley, and then toss with the spaghetti. Serve topped with more Parmesan, if desired.

Nutrition per serving: *304 calories, 8g fat, 37g carbs, 19g protein*

sides

I know a lot of folks focus on the main dish of a meal (hence why it's called the main dish), but I'm more of a side girl myself. At Thanksgiving, I skip the turkey and instead fill up my plate with all the deliciousness that's circled around the bird on the table. After all, I can always have a turkey sandwich later.

Many of the side dishes and snacks in this section are a wonderful mixture of party- and health-friendly. You don't have to skimp on flavor or the crowd-pleasing factor just because you want to serve healthier options. With Greek yogurt, you can turn even classically sinful side dishes into dishes that fit well into a healthy diet.

not-so-devilish
DEVILED EGGS

I come from a large family, and deviled eggs are a favorite holiday treat for all of us. As soon as the tray of eggs comes out of the fridge, we swarm around it and dive right in. I don't think a tray of eggs has ever actually made it to the appetizer table. In my version of this family favorite, mayo is out, and Greek yogurt and hummus are in. These are deviled eggs that don't need a special occasion.

 16 DEVILED EGGS   **10 MINUTES**

INGREDIENTS

8 hard-boiled eggs, peeled and sliced in half
2 tablespoons plain hummus
1/4 cup plain Greek yogurt
2 teaspoons Dijon mustard
1/8 teaspoon dried dill
Salt and pepper, to taste
Paprika, for garnish

DIRECTIONS

Remove yolks from the egg halves and place in a bowl. Mash with a fork. Add hummus, yogurt, mustard, dill, salt, and pepper. Stir until smooth. Transfer the filling to a piping bag and pipe into egg halves. Sprinkle tops of eggs with paprika for color.

SIDES AND SNACKS

114   *Nutrition per deviled egg: 35 calories, 2g fat, 1g carbs, 3g protein*

Deviled eggs are best served right after they are filled. For easy party prep, make the filling and stash it in a zip-top bag until you're ready to pipe. Then just snip off the corner and use that to pipe the filling into the egg halves.

*Feel free to play
with the yogurt—mayo
ratio in the dressing.*
I like half and half because it makes
it healthier without making it so
healthy that partygoers
are uninterested.

potato salad with SUNDRIED TOMATOES *and bacon*

There are a lot of great potato salads out there, but most of them are a variation on the same theme—potatoes and a mayo-based sauce. This potato salad kicks up the flavor by adding bacon, sun-dried tomatoes, and fresh herbs like thyme and sage. Every time I bring this salad to a potluck, I get rave reviews and lots of recipe requests.

 8 SERVINGS   **30 MINUTES (PLUS CHILLING TIME)**

INGREDIENTS

2 pounds potatoes, cut into bite-size chunks

1/2 cup finely diced onion (about 1 small)

1/2 cup plain Greek yogurt

1/2 cup mayonnaise

1 teaspoon Dijon mustard

2 tablespoons white wine vinegar

1/4 cup finely minced fresh sage

1 tablespoon finely minced fresh thyme

1/2 teaspoon kosher salt

1/2 teaspoon black pepper

4 slices bacon, cooked and crumbled

1/2 cup diced sun-dried tomatoes

DIRECTIONS

Add potatoes to a large stock pot and cover with a few inches of water. Bring to a boil over high heat. Cook until potatoes are fork-tender, about 15 minutes. Remove from heat and drain. Set aside. In a small bowl, combine onion, yogurt, mayo, mustard, vinegar, sage, thyme, salt, and pepper to make the dressing. In a large bowl, combine potatoes, bacon, and sun-dried tomatoes. Pour dressing over potato mixture and toss to combine. Refrigerate for 1 to 2 hours or until cold.

Nutrition per serving: 210 calories, 9g fat, 25g carbs, 7g protein

simple CUCUMBER & ONION salad

This quick, summery side dish is the first thing I always make when cucumbers and onions start coming out of the garden. The beauty of this salad is that there is just enough added flavor to really set off the freshness of the cukes and onions. Make sure you track down the freshest, sweetest cucumbers and onions you can find. You'll be rewarded!

YOU'LL NEED

2 medium cucumbers

1 large onion, sliced

1 cup plain Greek yogurt

2 tablespoons mayonnaise

1/4 cup white vinegar

1 teaspoon minced fresh dill

Salt and pepper to taste

Nutrition per serving: 95 calories, 3g fat, 13g carbs, 6g protein

Using a fork, scrape down the sides of each cucumber, creating grooves.

Slice the cucumbers into thin rounds.

Mix the cucumber and onion slices together in a large bowl.

In a smaller bowl, whisk together the yogurt, mayo, vinegar, dill, salt, and pepper.

Pour over cucumbers and onions. Toss to coat.

Refrigerate for 10 to 15 minutes to allow flavors to

Serve cold.

bok choy and apple GREEK YOGURT SLAW

This slaw is a unique twist on the classic picnic-table coleslaw. Instead of standard cabbage, it uses crunchy, flavorful bok choy and sweet shredded apple for an interesting mixture of textures and flavors.

 4 SERVINGS   **15 MINUTES (PLUS CHILLING TIME)**

INGREDIENTS

3 small heads bok choy (about 2/3 pound), julienned or shredded
1/2 small onion, julienned or shredded
1 small apple, julienned or shredded
1 large stalk celery, julienned or shredded
1 large carrot, julienned or shredded
1/3 cup plain Greek yogurt

1/3 cup sour cream
2 tablespoons white wine vinegar
1 tablespoon honey
1/2 teaspoon garlic powder
Salt and pepper, to taste
1 teaspoon poppy seeds

DIRECTIONS

In a large bowl, combine bok choy, onion, apple, celery, and carrot until well mixed. Set aside. In a medium bowl, whisk together the yogurt, sour cream, vinegar, honey, garlic powder, salt, and pepper. Pour dressing over bok choy mixture and toss to coat. Add in poppy seeds and toss to distribute. Pop in the fridge for 20 to 30 minutes before serving.

Nutrition per serving: 105 calories, 5g fat, 15g carbs, 2g protein

If you can't get your hands on bok choy, sub in a head of shredded green cabbage and up the celery stalks to 3.

Yukon Gold potatoes (and other gold-fleshed potatoes) have a much lower starch content than regular baking potatoes. This means that when they're cooking, they turn creamy and soft instead of crumbly and fluffy.

yogurt-chive SMASHED POTATOES

To make really great mashed potatoes, all you really need are potatoes, salt, and butter, but if you're looking for something a bit more adventurous, this yogurt-chive version is for you. The yogurt adds an incredible creaminess and tang that really sets off the warm, comfortable flavor of the potatoes.

 8 SERVINGS   **30 MINUTES**

INGREDIENTS

1/2 pound Yukon gold potatoes, peeled and diced
1/2 pound red new potatoes, halved or quartered
6 tablespoons (3/4 stick) butter
2 tablespoons minced chives
1/3 cup milk
2/3 cup plain Greek yogurt
Salt and pepper, to taste

DIRECTIONS

Place the potatoes in a large stock pot, and cover with water. Bring to a boil and simmer until potatoes are fork-tender, about 15 minutes. Drain and return to pot. Add the butter, chives, and milk, and mash using a potato masher until potatoes are smooth and no large chunks are left. Then mash in the yogurt, salt, and pepper.

I love the texture **and appearance of the peels of the red-skinned new potatoes in my mashed potatoes, but if you're a fan of perfectly smooth, just leave out the new potatoes and double the peeled Yukon Gold potatoes.**

Nutrition per serving: *127 calories, 8g fat, 12g carbs, 3g protein*

SIDES AND SNACKS

123

broccoli rice CHEDDAR BAKE

This comfort food dish is a perfect treat for a cold winter's night (or maybe just a dinner after a bad day at work). We eat this casserole as both a side dish and (after adding some cooked chicken breast) a main dish.

8 SIDE-DISH SERVINGS   **1 HOUR**

INGREDIENTS

1 1/2 cups brown rice

3 cups plus 1 1/2 cups chicken or vegetable stock

1 tablespoon butter

1 clove garlic, minced

1 small onion, diced

2 tablespoons flour

4 cups broccoli florets

1 1/4 cups shredded extra-sharp cheddar cheese

1/2 cup plain Greek yogurt

1/2 teaspoon salt

1/4 teaspoon pepper

1/2 cup panko bread crumbs

DIRECTIONS

Preheat oven to 350°. In a small saucepan, combine the rice and 3 cups of stock over high heat. Bring to a boil, reduce heat, cover, and simmer for 20 minutes, or until the liquid is absorbed. Remove from heat and let rest, covered, for 10 minutes. Set aside. Melt the butter in a large skillet over medium-high heat. Add in the garlic and onion, and cook until translucent and fragrant, about 4 minutes. Sprinkle the flour over the onion and garlic, and stir to coat. Pour in the remaining 1 1/2 cups of stock and the broccoli florets. Cook until the broccoli florets turn bright green and just begin to soften, about 5 minutes. Remove from heat, and stir in cheddar cheese, yogurt, salt, pepper, and prepared rice. Transfer the mixture to a 9 x 13-inch baking dish and sprinkle with panko bread crumbs. Bake for 25 to 30 minutes, or until the top is browned and the casserole is bubbly.

Nutrition per serving: *282 calories, 9g fat, 38g carbs, 12g protein*

I like the classic brown rice in this recipe, but it would also work well with other whole grains, like quinoa or farro.

pepperoni pizza
MAC AND CHEESE

This is probably one of the least healthy recipes in this book (although we've yet to make it to the dessert section). Even though this isn't the lightest of choices, it is definitely worth making for a special occasion—my husband likes to request this along with Maple-Bacon Burgers (page 101) for his birthday dinner every year. It's a great treat!

 8 SERVINGS   **45 MINUTES**

INGREDIENTS

13 ounces whole wheat
   elbow macaroni

2 tablespoons olive oil

3 tablespoons all-purpose flour

1 cup low-fat milk

1/2 teaspoon dried oregano

1/2 teaspoon dried basil

1/2 teaspoon dried parsley

1 cup low-fat cottage cheese

3/4 cup plain Greek yogurt

1/2 cup shredded fontina

1/2 cup shredded Romano

1/2 cup shredded mozzarella

3 ounces pepperoni,
   sliced into thin strips

1 medium tomato, diced

Salt and pepper, to taste

1/3 cup panko bread crumbs

DIRECTIONS

Preheat oven to 350°. Cook macaroni according to package directions, omitting salt and fat. Drain and set aside.

In a large saucepan, heat olive oil over medium-low heat. Whisk in flour and cook while constantly whisking for 3 minutes. Reduce heat to low. Slowly pour in milk while whisking, and whisk until well mixed. Add in oregano, basil, and parsley. Bring milk to a simmer, whisking frequently. Simmer for 5 to 6 minutes or until thickened. Remove from heat and let cool for 10 minutes. Then stir in cottage cheese, yogurt, fontina, Romano, and mozzarella until melted. Then add pepperoni, tomato, salt, and pepper.

Add cooked macaroni to the cheese sauce and toss to coat. Pour into a 9 x 13-inch baking dish. Sprinkle panko bread crumbs evenly on top. Bake for 15 to 20 minutes, or until edges are bubbly and bread crumbs are browned and crunchy.

The mixture of cheeses may sound a bit fussy, **but it's a great combo that melts beautifully and adds a ton of flavor. It's worth it to seek them out.**

Nutrition per serving:
527 calories, 20g fat, 58g carbs, 28g protein

I like using celery sticks for dippers with this, because volume is good. And I can eat celery all game long without wrecking my diet. But if you have party guests who aren't big celery fans, then pretzels and tortilla chips or pita chips work well as dippers, too.

buffalo blue cheese
CHICKEN DIP

Game-day party food is pretty much the opposite of healthy fare—which is fine if you are one of those amazing people who can pace yourself and only take one or two trips to the buffet table, but I'm not one of those people. When I'm watching sports, I want volume. I want to be able to snack through all four quarters without feeling like I need to run a marathon the next day to work it off. This dip is the best of both worlds—healthy and tasty. It's game-day deliciousness without any guilt.

 12 SERVINGS   **30 MINUTES**

INGREDIENTS

4 ounces Neufchâtel cheese, softened (often sold as 1/3 Less Fat Than Cream Cheese)

1/2 cup crumbled blue cheese

1 cup plain Greek yogurt

2 cups shredded cooked chicken breast

1/2 cup buffalo wing sauce (use more if you like it spicy; this amount is for a mild dip)

2 tablespoons chopped fresh parsley

1/2 cup shredded sharp cheddar cheese

1/2 teaspoon dried dill

1/2 teaspoon garlic powder

1/2 teaspoon onion powder

Salt and pepper, to taste

2 green onions, sliced thin

Celery sticks, for dipping

DIRECTIONS

Preheat oven to 350°. In a large bowl, mix together the Neufchâtel cheese, blue cheese, yogurt, shredded chicken, buffalo sauce, parsley, cheddar, dill, garlic powder, onion powder, salt, and pepper until well combined. Pour mixture into an ungreased 1-quart casserole dish. Bake for 15 to 20 minutes, or until the dip is bubbly and the top is beginning to brown. Sprinkle green onions on top and serve immediately with dippers.

Nutrition per serving: 113 calories, 8g fat, 2g carbs, 8g protein

eight-layer
FIESTA DIP

1/2 cup salsa

1 (16 ounce) can refried beans

1 package taco seasoning

2 1/4 cups plain Greek yogurt

1 cup guacamole

3 Roma tomatoes, diced

1/4 cup diced onions

1 cup shredded sharp cheddar cheese

1/2 cup sliced black olives

1/4 cup chopped cilantro

Versions of this crowd-pleasing layered dip have been floating around the party circuit for years. This particular recipe is a bit on the lighter and healthier side, but still packs a ton of flavor. Serve it with a big bowl of thick-cut, restaurant-style tortilla chips for dipping.

Nutrition per serving: 194 calories, 11g fat, 15g carbs, 11g protein

1. In a mixing bowl, stir together the refried beans, salsa, and 1/4 cup of the yogurt.

2. Spread the bean mixture in the bottom of a trifle dish or other clear bowl.

3. In another mixing bowl, mix together the remaining yogurt and the taco seasoning.

4. Spread the yogurt mixture on top of the refried beans.

5. Spread the guacamole on top of the yogurt mixture.

6. Layer on the tomatoes and

7. Sprinkle on the cheese, olives, and cilantro. Top with another dollop of yogurt, if desired.

8. Serve with plenty of tortilla chips for

SIDES AND SNACKS

131

quick and easy
VEGETABLE DIP

I love vegetables as much as the next healthy girl, but sometimes they can be a little bit blah, don't you think? There are tons of vegetable dip recipes out there, but a lot of them totally negate the health factor of eating fresh vegetables in the first place. This recipe is for a vegetable dip you can eat anytime.

 4 SERVINGS   **10 MINUTES**

INGREDIENTS

2 cups plain Greek yogurt

1/4 cup mayonnaise

1/4 cup dried onion flakes

1/4 cup dried parsley

1 tablespoon garlic powder

1 teaspoon celery seeds

2 teaspoons dried dill

1 teaspoon salt

1/2 teaspoon black pepper

DIRECTIONS

Combine all ingredients in a small bowl. Serve immediately with carrots, celery, or other vegetable dippers.

Nutrition per serving: *132 calories, 5g fat, 12g carbs, 10g protein*

SIDES AND SNACKS

This recipe works subbing in whole wheat flour for the all-purpose, too. But it does result in a crumblier, drier cornbread.

jalapeño–cheddar CORNBREAD

Cornbread can be quite the controversial topic. I know some folks who would have me arrested if they could for doctoring up cornbread with sugar, jalapeños, cheese, and Greek yogurt, but it's totally worth taking the heat if I get to eat this amazing bread. This cornbread is crumbly but still moist and has a ton of spice and tang. Cornbread purists, avert your eyes.

 12 SERVINGS   **45 MINUTES**

INGREDIENTS

1 cup fine-ground cornmeal

1 cup all-purpose flour

2 tablespoons sugar

1 cup frozen corn kernels

1/2 teaspoon baking soda

1/2 teaspoon salt

1 cup plain Greek yogurt

2 eggs

2 tablespoons butter, melted

1/3 cup milk

1/2 cup shredded sharp
  cheddar cheese

2 jalapeños, seeded and minced

DIRECTIONS

Preheat oven to 375°. In a large mixing bowl, whisk together the cornmeal, flour, sugar, corn kernels, baking soda, and salt. Make a well in the center of the mixture, and add in the yogurt, eggs, butter, and milk. Stir until just combined—do not overmix. Fold in the cheddar cheese. Spoon batter into a medium-sized cast-iron skillet or an 8 x 8-inch baking pan, and smooth the top with a spatula. Sprinkle on the jalapeños, and bake for 25 to 30 minutes, or until the top is browned and a toothpick inserted in the middle comes out mostly clean.

Nutrition per serving: *217 calories, 7g fat, 29g carbs, 9g protein*

desserts

*I*f you expected this dessert section to be chock-full of frozen yogurt recipes, you'll be pleasantly surprised to hear that the variety of ways you can use Greek yogurt for sweet treats goes far beyond fro-yo.

Greek yogurt is an amazing way to help lighten up even the most decadent of baked goods, and its creamy, rich texture lends itself to being a perfect centerpiece for all kinds of sweet treats.

And if you do happen to be a frozen-yogurt fan, you'll find some fun twists on your normal flavors, too. I personally love the No-Ice-Cream-Maker-Needed Cookie Dough Frozen Yogurt (page 154); it's a breeze to make and, like the title says, requires no special equipment.

YOGURT ICE POP

It doesn't get much simpler (or healthier!) than these tropical frozen treats. If you don't have a ice pop mold, you can use small paper cups with aluminum foil on top and ice pop sticks. The aluminum foil will hold the stick while the pop freezes.

 6 ICE POPS   **5 MINUTES (PLUS FREEZING TIME)**

INGREDIENTS

1/2 cup plain Greek yogurt
1/2 large ripe banana
1/2 cup canned pineapple chunks
1/4 cup milk
2 to 4 tablespoons honey

DIRECTIONS

Combine all ingredients in the jar of a blender. Blend on high until the mixture is very smooth. Taste test for sweetness and add more honey if necessary. Divide evenly into an ice pop mold. Freeze 4 to 6 hours or until solid.

DESSERTS

Nutrition per serving: 50 calories, 0.3g fat, 11g carbs, 2g protein

If you have a really ripe, spotted banana, you might be able to skip adding honey all together. Just taste the mixture before you add it in.

swirly twirly FRUIT AND YOGURT *ice pops*

I love these ice pops because they are totally customizable. Here I used strawberries and blueberries, which make a pop perfect for serving at your patriotic barbecue in July, but you can use whatever fruit you and your family love.

YOU'LL NEED

4 cups plain Greek yogurt

1 tablespoons vanilla extract

1/4 cup to 1/2 cup honey

3 cups fruit of choice
(I used 1 1/2 cups blueberries and 1 1/2 cups strawberries)

Nutrition per serving: 96 calories, 0g fat, 18g carbs, 6g protein

1

In a small bowl, whisk together the yogurt, vanilla extract, and 1/4 cup of the honey. Set aside.

2

In the jar of a blender, combine fruit and desired amount of remaining honey (little or none for sweet fruits), and blend until smooth. If using multiple kinds of fruit, do them in separate batches.

3

Using a spoon or spatula, press the fruit puree through a fine mesh sieve to remove any skins or seeds. Set aside.

4

Alternating between the puree(s) and the yogurt, layer evenly into paper cups, keeping in mind that the yogurt is the base and the fruit puree is an accent.

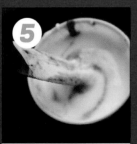

5

Gently swirl each cup using a knife to create a mixed and marbled texture.

6

Cover each cup with aluminum foil and insert an ice pop stick.

7

Freeze for 3 to 4 hours, or until solid.

8

To enjoy, tear top of paper cup and unwrap until pop comes out easily. Use the cup as a rest for your pop when you need a break from brain freeze. Or dip the cup in warm water and gently pull the pop out.

Nonfat Greek yogurt is just a touch too runny to make this mousse as creamy and decadent as I want it. Low-fat works well, but for the best texture, use whole-milk yogurt.

orange salted CHOCOLATE MOUSSE

Decadent, rich, and perfectly smooth, this orange-scented mousse can be served to even your most discerning dinner guests.

 6 SERVINGS   **15 MINUTES (PLUS CHILLING TIME)**

INGREDIENTS

8 ounces semisweet chocolate, chopped
3/4 cup low-fat milk
4 tablespoons granulated sugar
1 teaspoon vanilla extract
Juice and zest of 1 orange
1 tablespoon orange liqueur (optional)
2 cups plain whole or low-fat Greek yogurt
Coarse ground salt

DIRECTIONS

In a medium saucepan over medium-high heat, melt the chocolate with the milk and sugar until completely smooth. Remove from heat and whisk in the vanilla, orange juice and zest, and orange liqueur, if using. Set aside. Place the yogurt in a large mixing bowl. Slowly pour the chocolate mixture into the yogurt, using a spatula to fold it in. Keep folding until the chocolate is completely incorporated and no swirls remain. Transfer into serving dishes and refrigerate for 2 hours, or until cold. Serve topped with a small sprinkle of coarse salt.

Nutrition per serving: *299 calories, 13g fat, 40g carbs, 9g protein*

RASPBERRY YOGURT

key lime pie with

topping

One of my biggest weaknesses is a creamy, cool Key lime pie. It's tied to a particular vacation I took to Florida. I'm too ashamed to admit how much pie I ate during that trip, but I will tell you that was the moment I decided I needed to try my hand at my own version of this dessert.

 8 SERVINGS **45 MINUTES (PLUS CHILLING TIME)**

INGREDIENTS

1 1/2 cups graham cracker crumbs

3 tablespoons butter, melted

1 3/4 cups plain Greek yogurt

1 (14 ounce) can sweetened condensed milk

1 cup Key lime juice

3 eggs

Pinch of salt

1/4 cup confectioner's sugar

1/2 cup fresh raspberries, mashed

DIRECTIONS

Preheat oven to 375°. In a small bowl, mix together the graham cracker crumbs and butter. Press the mixture into a 9-inch pie plate to form a crust. Bake for 10 to 15 minutes, or until the crust is golden brown. Remove from oven and set aside. In a large mixing bowl, whisk together 3/4 cup of the yogurt, the sweetened condensed milk, lime juice, eggs, and salt until smooth. Pour into prepared crust and bake for 25 to 30 minutes, or until the pie is set. Let cool completely.

Meanwhile, in another large mixing bowl, whisk together the remaining yogurt, the confectioner's sugar, and mashed raspberries until smooth. Spread over cooled pie. Chill pie for at least 2 hours before serving.

Nutrition per serving: *360 calories, 11g fat, 54g carbs, 11g protein*

DESSERTS

This pie is decidedly rich and sweet, which means that a small slice goes a long way. Feel free to slice it into thin slivers for a lighter treat.

chocolate peanut–butter PRETZEL PIE

I'm definitely more of a pie girl than a cake person. My husband and I even had a pie bar at our wedding (and no wedding cake, thank you very much). I love a good fruit pie, but my favorite pies are ones that involve chocolate. And this definitely fits in that category.

 8 SERVINGS

 20 MINUTES (PLUS CHILLING TIME)

INGREDIENTS

Crust

2 cups pretzel twists, crushed into crumbs

3 tablespoons brown sugar

2 tablespoons unsweetened cocoa powder

3 tablespoons butter, melted

Filling

3 tablespoons cold water

1 package unflavored gelatin

1/2 cup milk

2/3 cup peanut butter

1 cup brown sugar

2 cups plain Greek yogurt

1 teaspoon vanilla extract

1/2 cup semisweet chocolate chips

1/2 cup milk

DIRECTIONS

Preheat oven to 350°. In a mixing bowl, combine the pretzel crumbs, brown sugar, cocoa powder, and butter until well mixed. Press the mixture into a 9-inch pie plate using clean, damp hands, making sure to form a crust along the sides of the plate as well. Bake for 10 minutes, or until the crust begins to brown. Set aside. Meanwhile, pour the water into a large mixing bowl, sprinkle the gelatin on top, and let rest for 5 minutes, or until the gelatin has absorbed the water and become jelly. Add the milk, peanut butter, brown sugar, yogurt, and vanilla to the gelatin mixture and whisk until smooth. Pour this mixture into the prepared crust. Cover tightly with plastic wrap and chill in the refrigerator until the gelatin filling is set, about 2 hours. Meanwhile, in a small saucepan over low heat, combine the chocolate chips and milk, and stir until the chocolate chips are melted. Remove from heat and drizzle over the chilled pie. Cut into 8 slices and serve.

Nutrition per serving:
400 calories, 20g fat, 44g carbs, 15g protein

Unflavored gelatin is a pantry staple in my kitchen.

I don't use it very often, but when I do, it's nice to have it there and ready to go.

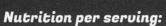

lemon poppy seed
CUPCAKES

Greek yogurt added to cakes makes them rich, dense, and totally moist—a combo that works really well in these citrusy cupcakes. Leave off the lemon buttercream frosting and you might even be able to pass these off as muffins at the breakfast table.

 12 SERVINGS   **40 MINUTES (PLUS COOLING TIME)**

INGREDIENTS

Cupcakes

1 1/2 cups granulated sugar
1 cup plain Greek yogurt
3 eggs
Juice and zest of 2 lemons
2 tablespoons butter, melted
1 teaspoon vanilla extract
2 cups all-purpose flour
2 tablespoons baking powder

Pinch of salt
1 tablespoon poppy seeds

Frosting

1/2 cup (1 stick) butter, softened
2 1/2 cups confectioner's sugar
2 tablespoons lemon juice
1/2 teaspoon vanilla extract
Pinch of salt

DIRECTIONS

Preheat oven to 350°. Fill the cups of a muffin tin with cupcake liners or spray with cooking spray, and set aside. In the bowl of a stand mixer, whisk together the sugar, yogurt, eggs, lemon zest and juice, butter, and vanilla. In a separate mixing bowl, combine the flour, baking powder, and salt. Add the dry ingredients to the wet in two batches, mixing until combined after each addition. Fold in the poppy seeds. Spoon the batter into the prepared muffin tin, filling the cups two-thirds full. Bake for 12 to 15 minutes, or until a toothpick inserted into the center of the cupcake comes out clean. Remove from oven and let cool completely. To prepare the frosting, whisk together the butter and sugar in a stand mixer until smooth. Then add in the lemon juice, vanilla, and salt, and continue to whisk at high speed until light and fluffy. Pipe or spread onto cooled cupcakes.

Nutrition per serving: 395 calories, 12g fat, 69g carbs, 5g protein

YOGURT CAKE

This cake lives in the holy land between the best chocolate cake and the best brownie you've ever had. It's moist, dense, and so rich that you only need a tiny sliver to satisfy your chocolate craving.

 16 SERVINGS   **1 HOUR**

INGREDIENTS

Cake
6 tablespoons butter, softened
1 1/2 cups granulated sugar
2 eggs
1 1/2 cups all-purpose flour
1 cup unsweetened cocoa powder

1 1/2 teaspoons baking powder
1/2 teaspoon baking soda
1/2 teaspoon salt
1 cup plain Greek yogurt
1/4 cup milk
1 tablespoon vanilla extract

Glaze
4 ounces bittersweet chocolate, chopped
3 tablespoons butter, softened
1/4 cup milk
1/2 cup confectioner's sugar

DIRECTIONS

Preheat oven to 350°. Grease a Bundt pan and set aside. In the bowl of a stand mixer, cream together the butter and granulated sugar until light and creamy. Add in the eggs and mix until combined. Then add in the flour, cocoa, baking powder, baking soda, and salt, and mix on medium-high until incorporated. Add in the yogurt, milk, and vanilla, and mix on medium until incorporated, then beat on high for 1 minute. Spread the batter evenly into the prepared Bundt pan. Bake for 35 to 40 minutes, or until a toothpick inserted into the cake comes out clean. Remove from oven and let cool completely in the pan. Once cool, flip out onto a plate and set aside.

To prepare glaze, combine the bittersweet chocolate, butter, and milk in a small saucepan over medium heat. Stir mixture until chocolate is melted. Remove from heat and stir in the confectioner's sugar until glaze is smooth. Pour over cake.

Nutrition per serving: 259 calories, 10g fat, 40g carbs, 6g protein

I'm an unabashed chocoholic, but if a dark chocolate cake with a dark chocolate glaze is a little much for you, an orange glaze would be great on top, too. To make, just whisk together 1/4 cup orange juice and 1/2 cup confectioner's sugar.

Greek yogurt cheesecake is a bit softer in texture than regular cheesecake. Make sure to cool the bars completely before you slice them.

strawberry swirl CHEESECAKE BARS

It's no surprise that Greek yogurt makes a great substitute for cream cheese when making cheesecake. These little cheesecake bites are smooth, flavorful, and perfect for serving at a party. All the crowd-pleasing flavor of cheesecake without any of the mess or fuss of cutting slices. Yum!

 16 SERVINGS   **40 MINUTES (PLUS COOLING TIME)**

INGREDIENTS

1 1/2 cups graham cracker crumbs

2 tablespoons brown sugar

6 tablespoons (3/4 stick) butter, melted

2 cups plain Greek yogurt

1 1/3 cups granulated sugar

2 eggs

1 teaspoon vanilla extract

1 tablespoon cornstarch

Pinch of salt

1/2 cup fresh or frozen strawberries

DIRECTIONS

Preheat oven to 375°. In a mixing bowl, combine the graham cracker crumbs, brown sugar, and butter. Pour the mixture into a 9 x 13-inch baking dish and press into bottom to form a crust. Set aside. In another mixing bowl, whisk together the yogurt, 1 cup of the sugar, the eggs, vanilla extract, cornstarch, and salt. Pour mixture on top of the prepared crust, and set aside. In a small saucepan over medium-high heat, mix together the strawberries and remaining sugar. Bring to a boil, reduce heat, and simmer until thick and bubbly, about 10 minutes. Remove from heat, and mash remaining whole strawberries using a potato masher or the back of a spoon. Drizzle the strawberry mixture on top of the yogurt mixture, and swirl using a knife. Bake bars for 30 to 35 minutes, or until the cheesecake is set. Remove from oven and let cool for 20 minutes at room temperature, then refrigerate for an additional 2 hours or until cold. Slice and serve.

Nutrition per serving: *167 calories, 6g fat, 26g carbs, 4g protein*

COOKIE DOUGH FROZEN YOGURT

I absolutely adore my ice-cream maker, but sometimes you just want some frozen yogurt without all the fuss of any added machinery. This recipe is for those times. It's basically an egg-free cookie dough recipe that you pop in the freezer for a few hours. After it's been through the chiller, it scoops like a perfect batch of frozen yogurt made in the most expensive ice-cream maker—no gadgets required.

 8 SERVINGS   **10 MINUTES (PLUS CHILLING TIME)**

INGREDIENTS

1/2 cup (1 stick) butter, softened
3/4 cup packed brown sugar
1/3 cup granulated sugar
1 tablespoon vanilla extract

1 cup all-purpose flour
1/4 teaspoon salt
3/4 cup chocolate chips or chocolate chunks
1 cup plain Greek yogurt

DIRECTIONS

In the bowl of a stand mixer, cream together the butter, brown sugar, and granulated sugar until smooth. Add in the vanilla, flour, and salt, and mix until combined. Then add in the chocolate chips and yogurt, and mix until combined. Spoon the mixture into a freezer-safe, airtight container and freeze until solid, about 2 hours.

Nutrition per serving: 344 calories, 16g fat, 44g carbs, 5g protein

Sometimes I serve this frozen yogurt as a side to a slice of warm Dark Chocolate Yogurt Cake (page 150). It's like a brownie sundae!

mint julep FROZEN YOGURT

I have to admit, bourbon isn't my favorite of liquors in mixed drinks, but I do have a special spot in my heart for bourbon as a flavor note in desserts. There is something about the warm, fiery taste that bourbon gives to desserts that is absolutely irresistible. A mint julep on its own can be a bit boozy for my tastes, but this sweeter, lighter take on the classic Southern cocktail is much more my style.

 **8 SERVINGS**   **15 MINUTES (PLUS PROCESSING AND CHILLING TIME)**

INGREDIENTS

3/4 cup bourbon
1/2 cup packed fresh mint leaves
1 cup sugar

3 cups plain low-fat Greek yogurt
1/2 teaspoon peppermint extract (optional)

DIRECTIONS

In a small saucepan over medium heat, combine 1/2 cup of the bourbon, mint leaves, and sugar. Bring to a boil, reduce heat, and simmer until the sugar is dissolved and the mint has infused into the bourbon, about 10 minutes. For better minty flavor, try tearing or muddling the mint leaves before boiling to release some of the natural oils. Remove the mint and discard. In a mixing bowl, combine the bourbon mixture, yogurt, and peppermint extract, if using (only use if your mint leaves are weak; the flavor of the mixture should be just slightly minty, but mint varies from batch to batch). Chill mixture until completely cold, about 2 hours. Process yogurt in your ice-cream maker per the manufacturer's instructions, adding in the remaining 1/4 cup bourbon just before it is finished. Or, if you don't have an ice-cream maker, freeze in a large bowl, stirring every 10 to 15 minutes until frozen. This method will result in an icier frozen yogurt.

Nutrition per serving: 209 calories, 1g fat, 32g carbs, 5g protein

honest-to-goodness zest FROZEN YOGURT

It feels like a lot of frozen yogurt recipes are trying to be ice cream—fighting against the inherent tangy flavor of the yogurt. This one embraces the tang! A bit of a disclaimer, though—this yogurt is 100 percent for citrus fans. It's lemony. Like, *lemony* lemony. In the most amazing, strong, tart, sour, tangy, addictive kind of way. It's just barely sweet, and a perfect dessert for a 90 degree day.

 6 SERVINGS   **10 MINUTES (PLUS PROCESSING AND CHILLING TIME)**

INGREDIENTS

2 cups plain low-fat or whole-milk Greek yogurt
Juice and zest of 2 lemons
1 tablespoon vanilla extract
2/3 cup honey

DIRECTIONS

Whisk together all ingredients in a medium mixing bowl. Refrigerate to chill. Process yogurt in your ice-cream maker per the manufacturer's instructions. Or, if you don't have an ice-cream maker, freeze in a large bowl, stirring every 10 to 15 minutes until frozen. This method will result in an icier frozen yogurt.

DESSERTS

Nutrition per serving: *76 calories, 1g fat, 36g carbs, 7g protein*

If you aren't a fan of tart foods, add more honey. You could also always drizzle it on just before serving. Yum!

dark chocolate coconut
FROZEN YOGURT

The key to this yogurt recipe is using a mixture of both Greek yogurt and coconut milk as a base. Not only is the coconut milk lightly flavored, creamy, and thick, but it also helps balance out the tang of the yogurt. The end result is a frozen yogurt that is more like the texture and flavor of a decadent scoop of full-fat ice cream.

 **8 SERVINGS**   **15 MINUTES (PLUS PROCESSING AND CHILLING TIME)**

INGREDIENTS

1 (14 ounce) can light coconut milk

1/4 cup honey

2 teaspoons cocoa powder

1 tablespoon cornstarch

1/2 cup semisweet chocolate chips

1/2 cup dried, unsweetened coconut

Pinch of salt

1/2 teaspoon coconut extract
   (optional, for a fuller coconut flavor)

1 1/2 cups plain Greek yogurt

DIRECTIONS

In a medium saucepan, whisk together the coconut milk, honey, cocoa, and cornstarch until blended. Turn heat to medium-high and bring to a simmer. Remove from heat, stir in chocolate chips, coconut, coconut extract (if using), and salt. Continue stirring until chocolate chips have melted. Chill chocolate mixture in the fridge until completely chilled—about 3 hours. Once cold, whisk in the yogurt and then process yogurt in your ice-cream maker per the manufacturer's instructions. Or, if you don't have an ice-cream maker, freeze in a large bowl, stirring every 10 to 15 minutes until frozen. This method will result in an icier frozen yogurt.

Nutrition per serving: 198 calories, 12g fat, 22 carbs, 3g protein

acknowledgments

Writing your first cookbook is certainly an adventure, and I've been so fortunate to have an incredible group of people along on this food-filled ride with me.

To my team at The Countryman Press and W. W. Norton, thank you so much for taking a chance on an unknown food-obsessed girl from the middle of nowhere. I feel so fortunate to have teamed up with a group that trusts my writing, design, and photography style. Thank you for your patience and education. This journey has been a blast, and I can't wait to work with you all again.

To all the friends I met during my time as a student and staff member at Indiana University, thank you for broadening the horizons of a sheltered girl from the country. Thank you especially to all my former colleagues and friends at IU Communications; even though we aren't together anymore, your creativity and perseverance continue to keep me inspired. Go Hoosiers!

To my blog readers and blog friends, I will never be able to explain how grateful I am to each and every one of you. Thank you for giving me purpose, supporting me through every twist and turn, and helping me discover a passion I never knew existed. I wish I could bring each of you a cupcake.

To my brother, sisters, nieces, nephews, and in-laws, it's comforting to know that if I need something, I have a whole gaggle of people to count on. Having that kind of support gives me the courage to pursue my dreams. Thank you for being my emotional safety net.

To my parents, I know a lot of people feel like they have the best parents in the world, but I know for a fact that I do. Thank you both for never laughing in my face when I came home with pink hair or a crazy artsy-fartsy idea. Dad, thank you for always challenging me, protecting me, and teaching me how to be the best creative I can be. Mama, if everyone were a little more like you, the world would be such a better place. Thank you for making the kitchen such a warm and welcoming place in our house, and thank you for teaching me that kindness really does matter.

To my husband, thank you for doing the dishes after all my kitchen bombs and eating more Greek yogurt in the past few months than anyone should ever have to. Thank you for pushing me outside my comfort zone and seeing more in me than I could ever see in myself. Thank you for being you and for loving me.

index

about the author

By day, Cassie Johnston works as a graphic designer, but after hours, Cassie is obsessed with all things edible. This love of growing, cooking, and eating food led to a second career in food writing, photography, and recipe development.

Cassie is a champion for local and organic food and, along with her husband, runs a small hobby farm in Southern Indiana producing heirloom vegetables, cut flowers, and maple syrup. Cassie shares her passion for cooking and eating daily at her healthy recipe blog, Back to Her Roots (backtoherroots.com).

When Cassie isn't writing about vegetables, you can find her hiking through the beautiful Indiana countryside, enjoying craft beer, and daydreaming about next year's crops.